Super Service

Completely Revised and Expanded

Seven Keys to Delivering Great Customer Service
Even When You Don't Feel Like It
Even When They Don't Deserve It

Val Gee
Jeff Gee

New York Chicago San Francisco
Lisbon London Madrid Mexico City Milan
New Delhi San Juan Seoul Singapore
Sydney Toronto

2 3 4 5 6 7 8 9 0   QFR/QFR   1 5 4 3 2 1

ISBN: 978-0-07-162579-1
MHID: 0-07-162579-8

This publication is designed to provide accurate and authoritative information in regard to the subject matter covered. It is sold with the understanding that the publisher is not engaged in rendering legal, accounting, or other professional service. If legal advice or other expert assistance is required, the services of a competent professional person should be sought.
—*From a Declaration of Principles Jointly Adopted by a Committee of the American Bar Association and a Committee of Publishers and Associations*

McGraw-Hill books are available at special quantity discounts to use as premiums and sales promotions, or for use in corporate training programs. To contact a representative, please visit the Contact Us pages at www.mhprofessional.com.

This book is printed on acid-free paper.

For Syona and Armando—our joy and inspiration!

Contents

Introduction   1

PART I: THE BASICS   7

Chapter 1   The Heart of the Matter   9

Chapter 2   Serving Up Your Best (Even When Feeling Your Worst)   37

PART II: SEVEN KEYS TO DELIVERING SUPER SERVICE   49

Chapter 3   CUSTOMER SERVICE KEY 1: The Right Attitude   51

Chapter 4   CUSTOMER SERVICE KEY 2: Understand the Customer's Needs   63

Chapter 5   CUSTOMER SERVICE KEY 3: Communicate Clearly   75

Chapter 6   CUSTOMER SERVICE KEY 4: Reach Agreement   91

Chapter 7   CUSTOMER SERVICE KEY 5: Check Understanding   103

Chapter 8   CUSTOMER SERVICE KEY 6: Take Action   115

Chapter 9   CUSTOMER SERVICE KEY 7: Build on Satisfaction   129

PART III: ADVANCED CUSTOMER SERVICE SKILLS   139

Chapter 10   How to Handle an Unhappy Customer   141

Chapter 11   Selling Skills   159

Chapter 12   Telephone Skills   171

Chapter 13   How to Avoid Stress and Burnout   183

Index   200

About the Authors

Jeff Gee is a motivational speaker and master trainer with Motorola. He has over 30 years of experience in the business world, and he founded McNeil & Johnson, a management training company, in 1982. Today the company is a million-dollar firm with offices in the United States, Australia, Egypt, Guatemala, and the United Kingdom. Jeff wrote and self-published *Strategies for Winning*, a set including a manual and six audio tapes that sold over 20,000 copies. Jeff Gee trains and motivates groups of people almost every day. He travels regularly to Asia, Europe, Eastern Europe, South America, Australia, and extensively throughout the United States.

Val Gee is an educational specialist and ordained priest. Val has had a series of over 10 articles, entitled "Insight," published in *Training Magazine*.

Their various (self-published) training manuals have sold over 20,000 copies. The authors have an extensive client list that includes Siemens, Motorola, Abbott & Culligan International, 3Com, Platinum Technology, Crane International, Pitney Bowes, Baxter, Sears, and Hyatt Hotels. They are also the coauthors of *The Customer Service Training Kit*, *The Winners Attitude*, and *Open Question Selling*.

For more information, go to www.mjlearning.com.

Introduction

What are the benefits of delivering *Super Service*
from a customer service provider's point of view?

This revised and expanded edition of *Super Service* provides information that we include in our workshops about the three brains, the IKTA disease, Up-selling, and many more interesting tools that will help you provide *Super Service*. Please enjoy, and if you have any questions e-mail us at: coach@mjlearning.com. Or go to our Web site: www.mjlearning.com for more information about our programs.

In the first edition of this book we included an amazing story. Marty, a tollbooth operator, takes *Super Service* to the next level by smiling and greeting every single driver who stops at his booth. We gave the story to a group of customer service providers who argued, "While we want to do a good job, we don't see any future in it, and we would never put our 'soul' into the job!" They joked that they didn't want to be an "eternally smiling tollbooth operator" and that people like Marty are extremely rare. This was great feedback, because it made us return to some basic questions:

1. From a customer service provider's point of view, what are the benefits of delivering *Super Service*?
2. How will it make the life of a service provider easier, more fun, and more meaningful?
3. How will this book help providers who look at their jobs as *only jobs*, and who may be disillusioned, cynical, and tired of their work?

Not surprisingly, the answers to these questions are not based on the bottom line, productivity, or happy customers. They ultimately come from you, the customer service provider, because—wherever you go, whatever you do, however you feel—you cannot get away from yourself. This book is designed to help you find reserves of strength and joy in yourself that can help you enjoy giving *Super Service* to customers—even when you don't feel like it and even when they don't deserve it!

Think about it. It makes sense. Who gets to feel better after doing a good job? Who gets to experience fun when you make a customer laugh? Who gets to feel that work is more meaningful after helping a customer understand a system, learn something new, or grasp other things that your job consists of?

Your work as a service provider is critically important. A lot of research backs up this statement. That's why so many companies spend millions on marketing surveys that ask, "What do our customers want? How can we satisfy them?" The answers to these surveys are written up in customer service books directed toward marketing, sales, and management.

We, however, are more interested in how frontline customer service providers can deliver *Super Service* in a way that enriches their own lives, without feeling burned out at the end of the day. This book therefore defines the problems and answers that service providers—like you—come up against every day. We believe you can do a great job for yourself and your customers. *Super Service* is a positive philosophy on life.

If you don't believe it, read the story of Marty and ask yourself, "Does Marty feel good at the end of the day? Does it cost him anything? Does he make a difference in people's lives?" Here's Marty's story. See what you think!

Marty works on a very busy Illinois tollway and stands at the far left coin collection basket. His job is to watch cars go through, and that's what all the other operators do. They just watch! Whatever the weather (and it gets below freezing in Chicago), Marty stands by the coin basket. Sometimes it's raining so hard he looks like a fisherman with all of his wet gear on. What is different about Marty, though, is that thousands of drivers deliberately drive over 10 lanes of traffic just to go through his tollbooth.

Why? Well, if you keep your hand out after throwing in the coins, he gives you a high-five as you drive away. And if you whiz by without your hand out, he bends down, looks you in the eye, and calls out, "Hey, have a great day!" or "Make it a good one!"

We were so intrigued by him that one day we parked the car on the shoulder and walked over to him.

Gees:	"Do you have a couple of minutes?"
Marty:	"Well, I'm a bit busy," he said, nodding to the line of cars waiting to come through. (The barrier is left up in the mornings, so we weren't holding up traffic, but still . . .) "Sure!" he said.
Gees:	We got right to the point, "How come you're always so cheerful in the mornings?"
Marty:	"It's my job! *Have a good one!*" Marty called out, still attentive to his job.
Gees:	"But all the other operators just stand there. They don't acknowledge a single driver unless there's a problem."
Marty:	"It's their option in life, to do what they want to do. Mine is to be the best I can. I'm here to serve these people."
Gees:	"Why?"
Marty:	"I have to!" he said. Our blank faces told him we needed more information. "When I see all these drivers coming toward me looking so miserable and anxious, I feel it's my job to help them have a great day!"
Gees:	"How long have you been doing this?" we asked, thinking Marty would say a year at most.

Marty: "Twenty years."

Gees: "And all that time you've been giving high-fives and saying, 'Have a great day!'?"

Marty: "Yep."

Gees: "Okay, trick question: Are you like this at home?"

Marty: "Yep."

Marty wasn't trained or asked to serve people; he just assumed the role. Marty could have spent 20 years being miserable and thinking he didn't get paid to serve high-fives. His story is what *Super Service* is all about. It's more than putting yourself in the shoes of your customer. It's remembering that the customer is a human being, a person with a rent or mortgage to pay, kids to feed, a spouse, a mother, a father— a person with feelings just like you.

Marty could choose to think that his job is about working with a bunch of noisy, four-wheeled pollutants, that the line of cars coming toward him is just a never-ending machine. Instead he chooses to focus on the people within the cars; they are his customers. He recognizes their frustrations with the tollbooth: *They have to pay money to slow down!*

Marty has worked out that the best way to serve his customers is to make it worthwhile for them to slow down—even look forward to going through. His business proposition is that 40 cents is a small price to pay for the feel-good attitude he gives out. If you could talk with Marty, you would feel his self-worth. He's taken a job and upgraded it. He likes it and the customers like it. It's a win-win situation.

That's Marty's story and, yes, being a tollbooth operator is not everyone's cup of tea. However, if you were a tollbooth operator, would you want to be the happy one? The one who made a difference? The one whom people remembered? Marty represents what genuine service is all about: a person who cares about his job and believes his contribution can and will positively benefit others.

Perhaps your answer is still, "No! I wouldn't want to be happy in that job, because I might end up as a tollbooth operator for the rest of my life! I would rather be grumpy, miserable, and angry with the customers. Then my anger will force me to move on, or up, or somewhere else; anywhere but here!"

The problem is that it doesn't usually work like that. Have you noticed that grumpy people stay grumpy even if they are in the best job in the world? So, if you are really unhappy in your job, do yourself and your company a favor: Change jobs.

But here's the kicker: Try delivering *Super Service* in your current job while you look for another one. Call it a practice session. If you can deliver great service when you really don't feel like it and they don't deserve it, your whole life will change. And that's really what *Super Service* is all about: serving yourself a great life. So let's take a look at what *Super Service* can do for you.

HOW *SUPER SERVICE* WORKS FOR ME

1. *I experience being at my best.* When I deliver *Super Service*, the person who receives the most service is me.
2. *I am not at the mercy of my customers.* It doesn't matter if my customers deserve *Super Service* or not; by choosing to give it to them anyway, I am in control of how I feel.
3. *My life becomes easier, more fun, more meaningful.* When I feed the positive energy within me, it grows in all other aspects of my life, and positive energy attracts positive energy! (The same is true with negative energy.)
4. *People notice that I do a great job and I become an asset.* When I am tired of my work or see my job as just a job, I really want to move on. The problem is that it's hard to move on when I feel stuck in mental fatigue. If I change my attitude, my whole world is filled with new opportunities.

PART I

The Basics

The Heart of the Matter

Connecting with a customer's heart and soul means
experiencing your customers as fully rounded human beings with
all the joy, family issues, money scares, and work problems that
every one of us experiences from time to time.

Here is how two of our clients, who participated in our *Super Service* workshop, answered the following three questions:

Mary—McDonald's Corporation, Accounting

1. **As a customer, what do you want?**
   "I want to get a sense of being valued. I place more value on service than I do on the price tag. Yes, I'm frugal so if I've decided to buy the product, I will, but it's the service that makes me a repeat customer."

2. **As a customer, what do you feel stops you from getting what you want?**
   "People who just don't care or won't go the extra step. I will choose not to get the product if the person is not the right fit. I will get what I need somewhere else."

3. **In your experience, what do customer service people do best?**
   "They respect and listen to the customer. They give undivided time and attention. They make you feel valued, so you do not feel like a statistic."

Frank—GE Commercial Finance, Inside Sales

1. **As a customer, what do you want?**
   "I want to be listened to and shown empathy."

2. **As a customer, what do you feel stops you from getting what you want?**
   "Employees that simply don't care. Make excuses, don't listen and try to get you off the phone or out of their way as fast as they possibly can!"

3. **In your experience, what do customer service people do best?**
   "They listen, empathize, and take charge."

The IKTA Disease

Before you read any further, please be aware of the IKTA disease (I Know That Already). It is a disease that stops us from learning new things, because we truly believe we know everything already. Open up your mind, clear your head of what you think you know, and be prepared to learn something new.

Brain Talk

I give this talk in every *Super Service* class that I facilitate. It's the foundation of creating loyal customers, and more importantly, of having an amazing life; in which you are happy, full of joy, and have a sense of purpose about your life. So in a way, this section of the book is the most important because it talks about you. Everything you do, your reactions and behaviors, starts and stops in your brain. The human brain is amazing, and it consists of three sections. The first brain is the reptilian brain. On top of this is the limbic system, or the animal brain. And on top of the animal brain is the cerebral cortex, which is the human brain.

The reptilian brain sits in the base of your spine. It looks after your amazing body. It makes sure your heart is beating, your lungs are breathing, and your kidney is filtering out toxins. It makes sure that every function in your body is working so that you can live a full, rich, and purposeful life.

Without the reptilian brain, you would die. Let's face it, you would not last very long if you were in charge of your heart beating. It would go beat, beat, beat, beat, oh forget this, this is too much work. It's unfortunate that the only time you stop and think about how amazing your body is, is when something goes wrong. And, then it's sometimes too late to be thankful.

There are many things to be thankful for your body. Your body is an amazing machine and the reptilian brain looks after it all without you thinking about it. For instance, do you know your heart pumps three Olympic-size swimming pools of blood through you every year. There are six thousand miles of veins, arteries, and tubing making sure everything is traveling where it needs to go. Two million blood cells die every second to be replaced by two million new ones until the day you die. Within each blood cell there are four million molecules. Each of those molecules has an atom oscillating at ten thousand times a second. And all of this is happening so that you can go out there and do outstanding things.

You are so full of energy that the next time your city has a blackout you could run up to the electric company and say "plug me in"! Your body has so much potential that you could climb Mount Everest, if you wanted to. You could run a marathon at 80 years of age. Your body is capable of achieving many things and this entire system is all being looked after by your reptilian brain.

Do you remember being a child? You had so much energy you couldn't wait to get out of bed. You probably got up at five or six in the morning and immediately started doing things. You couldn't wait to play and learn new things. And you didn't want to go to bed because you had the most amazing experience "living the day." But all you heard from your parents and teachers were, "Sit still and be quiet." Now, you can't wait to get INTO bed. Now you want to take things easy and do as little as possible. And this is all because we are thinking different thoughts all the time, which brings me to the animal brain.

On top of the reptilian brain sits the limbic system, or the animal brain. It's into survival because that's what an animal does. It's a survival-only process called "flight or fight." An animal has two things it can do when faced with a problem—run away or fight. If it sees a smaller animal, it will kill it; if it sees a bigger one, it will escape. An animal is freaked out about everything. It doesn't have great thoughts. It doesn't fall in love. Have you ever seen a giraffe with a five-year plan? When was the last time you saw your dog volunteer? Animals don't like eye contact. Animals don't like to be seen. Animals keep a low profile and try to get through the day without being killed. That is your limbic system; it's there to help you survive.

But we are living in a day and age when you don't need the animal brain to kick in *all* the time. There's not a lot of things we have to run from or fight. We don't have to hunt out a cow in our grocery stores. Your boss isn't trying to eat you. We can actually enjoy our lives and operate from our human brain. In the animal brain, we literally come from fear. It is born in fear and it dies in fear.

▼

KEY POINT

Most of the time there is nothing to be fearful about. Most of the time, we are safe—we do not need to operate from the animal brain.

When you are in your animal brain and you are fearful it plays out in different human emotions like anger, depression, frustration, envy, and greed. All of these negative emotions come out when you live in the limbic system or the animal brain. It hates successful people and it doesn't think too highly of you either. It tells you that you are ugly, stupid, and that you'll never make it. It doesn't care about your health. Cigarette packages warn you that smoking clogs the arteries and causes heart attacks and strokes, yet your animal brain convinces you to smoke. "Other people may die because they smoke but not you, your lungs are huge." Alcohol? "Yes! You've had a hard day, plus it'll help you sleep." Exercise? "Who needs it?"

All you want to do when you are in your animal brain is survive the day. Everything is a problem. And what does your animal brain think of customers? "What do they want now?! I wish the phone would stop ringing. I can't wait to go home and relax because I've been working like a dog." That's a great expression, because most dogs I've seen don't work very hard. In fact, most animals I've seen sleep all day and do as little as possible. They eat, poop, and if they can, they reproduce. Now some of you are thinking, wow, what a wonderful life that would be! All I have to do is sleep, eat, poop, and reproduce? Except we are amazing human beings; we've been asked to do more. We've been asked to fall in love. We've been asked to imagine a better future. We've been asked to do outstanding things. You can't do that in your animal brain, it only wants to survive.

On top of the animal brain, we have the cerebral cortex with the crowning achievement of the frontal lobe. We are the only animals who have it. This human brain is capable of planning and creating. We can imagine the future and bring it into reality. We can literally achieve anything we put our mind to. How do we know? Because ordinary people are doing extraordinary things all of the time, all over the world. The human brain wants to love, be loved, and be happy. How many happy people do you know? How quickly does it take you to be happy and how quickly does it take you to be angry? There is a way to see which brain you are in. You are in the human brain when you are happy or when you are in love.

Everyone has been in love or thought they were in love. How long did it last? Well, some people say that things creep in like reality, life, and excuses. But, that's not what happens. No, what creeps in is the animal brain saying don't get too close, don't be too vulnerable, remember you could get killed. So keep your light low, keep them at a distance, don't trust them, and everything will be okay. But that's not the way to have relationships or live an amazing life. The human brain wants to love, be loved, and be happy. A human being has a dream and can make it come true.

▼

KEY POINT

When you operate from your human brain, you are able to accept, understand, and empathize with your customers. This connects you at a higher level— they get it that you've got it—that you are going to help them!

You are staggeringly amazing. The problem is we have this duality going on between the animal brain and the human brain. In between these two brains is the "reticular activating system." It's a tiny, white bone, like a toggle, that vibrates or flicks up and down between the limbic system and the cerebral cortex all day long. This is where the voices come into play. Everyone on the planet has voices in their heads which talk to them every second. Sometimes the voice comes from the animal brain and sometimes it comes from the human brain, depending where the reticular activating system is switched. How quickly does it take you to get angry or upset? That is how you know which brain you are in. Usually the first voice you hear is the human brain, which says, "Wow, I'll exercise today because it makes me feel good." It's immediately followed by the animal brain, which says, "No, no, no, don't do that, it'll kill you. Do it next week when you're feeling better. Plus, it's hard work and we hate hard work."

So you have these voices constantly telling you to do things and not to do things. To be amazing or not be amazing, and this is the problem we have as human beings. Which voice do we listen to? Which voice is the master? Most of us want to be amazing but our animal brain tells us otherwise. I'm too fat, I'm too thin, I'm too short, I'm too tall, my nose is too big, it's not big enough, I'm mathematically challenged.

Let's take a look at a typical Monday morning to see which brain you are operating from. The alarm goes off and the first thing you do is hit the snooze button. (Some of you will hit the snooze button five or six times before getting out of bed.) The first thoughts are, "I hate Mondays." Finally, you drag yourself into the bathroom, look in the mirror, and all you can see are the flaws—the fat belly and the wrinkles. This is how you start your day. You don't want to go to work. You get in the car and have some road rage. You expect to have a bad day and many problems. And if it wasn't for those darn customers you'd be the best salesperson, or customer support person in the world!

Or do your voices sound like this in the morning? "Yahoo! It's Monday! Awesome! I'm alive!" And then you leap out of bed full of energy, and skip into the bathroom. You look in the mirror and see a god or goddess. You blow yourself a kiss and sing your heart out in the shower.

▼

KEY POINT

Engage your human brain by being aware of it. When you are coming from love and acceptance, that's where you will be living your best life.

So we are either living in the animal brain or the human brain. And we have to train our animal brain. We have to use it when we need it, not when it wants to rule our life. You've seen trained dogs. The owner says a command and the dog follows. The dog sits, fetches, and rolls over. Have you seen a dog that is untrained? The dog jumps up on you, barks like a lunatic, has no discipline, and it's chaos. Train your animal brain and start to talk to yourself about how amazing you are because in the human brain you can literally achieve anything. Remember how animal trainers train their animals? They do it by giving them food, attention, and encouragement—because that's what works best.

I don't care where you come from, what your religion is, what your color is, what your past is, or what your parents did. When you are in the human brain, you can literally achieve anything. We know this because there are millions of stories about people who have come from the "wrong" backgrounds with the "wrong" education and are successful beyond their wildest dreams. Why, because they are in the human brain more than they are in the animal brain. They are passionate about their lives, and they want to be the very best they can be.

Watch what people are doing. Can you spot the people who are operating in their animal brains? When you are in a restaurant or driving, see if you can spot the people in their human brains. And I'm telling you there are a lot more people in their animal brains than you think. These people are frightened, worried, upset, and depressed. One of the biggest industries around the world focuses on the treatment for depression. The American pharmaceutical companies make billions and billions of dollars because people are popping little pills to make themselves feel better. I'm not really sure what they have to feel bad about, but the pills make them feel good. The problem is the pills can slow you down. Some people on pills don't know where they are in terms of awareness. I'm not saying that no one should take anti-depressant drugs, I'm just saying that not everyone needs them.

Which brain do you want to be in? It's your choice. What purpose does it serve to go around blaming people? Or be defensive or, worse, be complacent. It doesn't serve you at all. You have to take in the fact that you are amazing. Whatever other people are doing is their thing and that is fine. We all have our own opinions and we make different choices because that is life. Remember:

- I don't have to take it on board.
- I don't have to take it personally and get upset, worried, or miserable.

When customers show anger toward me:

- I will not react to them in a negative way.
- I will, instead, be there to help them.
- I will not defend myself or my company.
- I will not tell them they are wrong.
- I will not take their words personally and get upset.
- I will be there to help them because I am in my human brain.
- I will be there to serve them and to be amazing.

When you are in the human brain, you want to love, to be loved, and to be happy. You want to be challenged, to take risks, and to give. You actually want to volunteer. When you are in your animal brain, you never raise your hand. You think that somebody else should do it. But when you are in your human brain you are passionate, interested, and capable of achieving anything. Everyone reading this book is a winner and we're just here to remind you.

▼ KEY POINT

Remember, you are in charge of how you think and feel—you are in the power seat.

Watch your voices. The one that says you are too thin, too fat, too short, too tall, too ugly, or too dumb; don't pay it any particular attention. Talk to yourself and affirm your day. Start right now. Go to a mirror, look at yourself in the mirror, and say "you and I"—who is "you" and who is "I"? You are on your own, just you and a mirror! "You" is your animal brain and "I" is your human brain. They are both in your head watching you.

So you look at yourself and say, "You and I, just for today, are going to be amazing. I don't need to be in survival mode and feel negative emotions. You and I are going to work together to have an amazing day. We are going to sing in the shower because it feels good! When I get stuck in traffic, instead of getting frustrated I'll sing to myself or wave to the other people. When I get to work, I am going to be the best they've ever seen. I'm going to have at least three people say, 'Wow, you look really happy!'"

That's what you need to do. You need to talk to yourself constantly. Why? Because of habits and routines, it's easy to forget, and we forget instantly, how amazing we are. You are in charge of your state of mind. You need to tell yourself you are talented, fabulous, smart, caring, sharing, and loving. You, yes you, you are amazing. I don't care about your past or any of the things you have done, or not done because, right now, you are perfect just the way you are.

We've talked to many successful people and this is what they do. They affirm their day. They talk to themselves about how amazing they are. They visualize their day:

- Maybe people are going to say bad things about me or to me.
- Maybe people are going to bring major problems to my doorstep, and it's okay. That's life.
- I am going to handle all of it with grace and compassion because I am a human being. And it's my choice how I deal with my life.

No more animal brain. Just go to the higher level. It's called "transcending." You have to transcend, end the trance of being in the animal brain, and start to be amazing. Just today. Just start with today. And once you keep doing that, affirming your day every day, the animal brain says, "Fine, I'll work with you, not against you." "I'll help you instead of hinder you." And pretty soon everything you do will be amazing.

Your thoughts and your feelings make everything happen. If you wake up worried, miserable, or depressed, guess what you are going to see? Worried, miserable, and upset people. If you wake up feeling good and ready for the day, telling yourself to relax and let things roll off your back, that's what will happen.

Every time you think and feel something from a place of awareness, you own it and it makes up your life. You can literally change what you do. You can make different choices. You will always be you, but you can make different choices starting right now. Right now. You can make your life better by doing things differently. The worst thing that will happen is your life will stay the same. The best thing that will happen is your life will get better and better and better. Even if your life is great now, it will get better. You'll meet new and interesting people, and have new and exciting experiences by switching from your animal brain to your human brain. Go for it. Take hold of that responsibility and accountability for being in your human brain and I promise magic will happen.

CHECK-IN

To be effective as a customer service provider, you need to operate from your human brain. In the spaces below, please list the emotions that correspond with the animal brain or the human brain.

Animal Brain	**Human Brain**
Anger	*Joy*

ACTION: HOW DO I KEEP IN MY HUMAN BRAIN

Affirm my day.

Keep a gratitude journal.

Sing in the shower.

Smile often.

Facilitate a positive environment.

Accept yourself and others.

Practice being patient.

Write down the positive actions you want to achieve today. _____

_____

I will operate from my human brain today by _____

_____

This book has everything you need to know about delivering great customer service. One of the most important things you will learn is this: "My customer is anyone who isn't me." This lesson is so critical to you as a professional *Super Service* provider that it's worth repeating: **My customer is anyone who isn't me!** This definition of customers includes all the people inside and all the people outside your company: internal and external customers.

Too often, we think of customers as targets: people to be haggled with, sold to, or serviced like a washing machine. In reality, customers are people and people have relationships. How's this for a relationship builder?

▼

KEY POINT

You may not always see your internal customers, but they are the people who benefit or suffer from the way you work.

Here's your drink, and I hope it chokes you!

This is a response from a fast-food server who was fed up with a customer who dared to complain about the slow service. Did the server really hope the drink would choke the customer? Probably not; it was just a mindless thing to say. That's the problem with service: We get so bored that our mind goes off somewhere else, and when we do that, we stop serving the customer. Words tumble out of our mouths and, before we know it, we've created a situation.

If we served people the way we want to be served, we wouldn't have "situations." The problem is that most of us don't want to serve. We think that "serve" is a nasty word—something we did to make our way through high school or college. In the real world we think, *"It's not my job to serve people, I want people to serve me!"*

One of the many definitions of the word *serve,* however, is "to be of assistance, to help." Most of us want to help, but only if we are in the mood, if we like the person, or if we feel serving will advance our cause in some way. The secret weapon for fighting this attitude is to *wake up*.

You may say, "I am awake, so this doesn't apply to me!" In the *Super Service* definition, "waking up" means being conscious of the fact that we are all in the *soup of life* together. It means opening our eyes wide in the morning and saying, "Yippee, I'm still on the planet!"

Maybe certain people we hate at work just reflect a negative behavior pattern that we hate in ourself, and that's why we don't like being around them. "Waking up" means asking yourself the question, "What if I change my attitude for a second and give that person a break?"

To give other people a break seems like a very hard thing to do; if we give them an inch, they might take a yard. Eventually that yard will turn into a mile and there'll be nothing left of me! Help! Where did I go?

Here's how waking up helps you: When you give someone a break, you are really giving yourself a break! Most of the time when we see a person we dislike, we think, "This person never smiles. He must dislike me a lot. I've seen him smile at other people." This thought gets louder over time. *"He never smiles at me. He must hate me, so I'm going to hate him back!"*

What happens then is really interesting. We become a mirror image of that person. We stop smiling at him, and we treat him as if he had the Ebola virus. In other words, we reflect his behavior back to him, and so the cycle continues.

Waking up means that we can break the cycle. We begin by noticing how we behave with other people. We notice that a person might just find it hard to smile, and we can decide to smile at the person anyway. If we don't get a response, it's okay because we want to be the kind of person who smiles.

What if *you* don't like to smile? Here's another example: "I hate that person because she always puts on a fake smile. She looks really dumb." When you see that person, you probably fake a smile back to her (and maybe even make an ugly face after she walks by). Again, it's a mirror image, and you end up with a fake smile plastered all over your face. So what do you do?

You could decide either to scowl at her or change the recipe: Speak to her. "Hey, I keep seeing you around and we've never met. I'd like to introduce myself." The moment you do this, you've woken up. You've broken the cycle of unfriendliness. It's a liberating feeling!

Domino's Pizza took the power of smiling to heart when they embarked on a new marketing campaign with a slogan, "A Million Smiles a Day." The campaign was grounded in simple, old-fashioned marketing fundamentals that said courtesy and friendliness go a long, long way. Domino's Pizza realized that their products, delivery, and services bring them face-to-face with many customers; so why not deliver a smile with every pizza!

Giver or Taker

Super Service professionals are great salespeople. They understand that to serve feels good and that it gets the job done. They have the attitude, "If I serve you, we both win."

You could say, "I don't get paid by commission. Why should I work harder and not get paid for it?" In a strict sense that response is true. You may not get more money today, but chances are that, when you change your pattern of behavior, everything will change, including your money. More importantly, you'll feel a whole lot better about yourself and your job.

Serving is about being a *giver* instead of a *taker*. If you think about it, we all serve other people. Even the most influential people in the world have to serve someone, even if it's a group of stockholders. Take a deep breath and hold it. Let the answer "pop" into your mind when you ask yourself this question: "Am I a *giver* or a *taker*?" Exhale. Whatever your answer, you get to choose how to react to this question. You can choose to think positive thoughts or negative thoughts. Here are some examples:

Positive Thoughts

I enjoy being a *giver* because I like to help people.

I enjoy being a *taker* because I like to receive.

Negative Thoughts

I hate being a *giver* because I don't get anything back.

I hate being a *taker* because people don't like me.

Sometimes, people take because they feel they have nothing to give. If your job is to answer customer complaints all day long, you need to give yourself breaks during the day. Revitalize your energy by taking a walk, reading a book, or having a five-minute break to chat with a friend or colleague.

▼

KEY POINT

Don't think this book is about giving until you feel wiped out and have no strength left. We have to give to ourselves in order to give to others. It's a question of balance. *Take care of yourself, too!*

A client once asked us to support him by calling him an hour after lunch to remind him to take a break. But he never answered his phone, so we told his voice mail to take a break and hoped he listened to his messages before he went home!

We all need to take breaks. Here are 20 suggestions that will help you to revitalize your energy.

20 WAYS TO REVITALIZE YOUR ENERGY

1. Have a piece of fruit.
2. Drink a glass of water.
3. Stretch your neck very slowly, backwards, forwards, side to side.
4. Lift your legs and circle your feet clockwise and counterclockwise.
5. E-mail a friend.
6. Tidy your desk and/or drawers.
7. Empty your wastebasket and remove clutter from the floor.
8. View your space from a distance and make improvements.
9. Read a newspaper.
10. Read an uplifting quote.
11. Lift your shoulders to your ears, make them tense, and then let go.
12. Take a short walk outside.
13. Take a bathroom break and walk a different route.
14. Hold your breath, and then release all your tension.
15. Close your eyes and visualize your favorite spot to be.
16. Record an uplifting message on your voice mail.
17. Call your home telephone and leave an uplifting message.
18. Start a journal and write a page a day.
19. Complete the sentence, "The insights I have about my life are . . ."
20. Complete the sentence, "What I need to do to be happy is . . ."

Everybody Serves Somebody

Question: Who serves?

Answer: Movie stars, *Super Service* providers, bankers, presidents, CEOs, kings, queens, generals, doctors, lawyers, etc.

Question: Do they feel their life is run by their customers?

Answer: Probably at times, yes.

Question: Do they ever get tired of their customers?

Answer: Probably at times, yes.

We all serve and we all get tired of it. That's okay; it's *how* we serve most of the time that makes for a happy or an unhappy life. We might think, "I will serve this person, and sometimes another person, but I will never serve that person!" The problem with this kind of thinking is that we judge who gets served and who doesn't. What if we are wrong? On a purely material level, what if the person we would never serve becomes our boss? Do we leave the company?

Doesn't it make sense to be of service to whoever needs it at the time? (That isn't to say that we become the company server!)

The Bottom Line of *Super Service*

One company did a landmark experiment that proves for all time the value of providing *Super Service*. The company was a manufacturer of building products. Their customers were 45,000 large building contractors. Their traditional methods: publish an annual catalog, mail it out, and wait for the phone to ring. The company was very profitable.

A management consulting firm suggested an experiment. Let's take the top 1,200 customers and divide them into two exactly equal groups: 600 in a test group, and 600 in a control group. The control group we will treat exactly as we treat all of our other customers. We will wait for the phone to ring, and be very nice to them when they call.

For the test group, we will use outbound relationship building. They assigned one customer service specialist and one building products engineer for the six-month test. These two people called every decision maker, influencer, and products user they could find in the 600 test companies. They did not try to sell. They did not offer discounts. They tried friendship and providing information. In summary, what they did was to:

- Ask about customers needs
- Follow up on bids and quotes
- Schedule product training
- Remind them of pricing specials
- Give product comparison information
- Give new product information and samples

What was the difference between the purchases made by the control group and the test group after six months?

- The test group made 12 percent more orders than they had in the previous six months.
- The control group made 18 percent fewer orders.
- The test group placed 14 percent larger orders, the control group 14 percent smaller orders than before.

In total, the test group bought products worth $2.6 million more than the control group during the six-month period. The total cost of the test was about $50,000. How's that for a return on investment?

The Cost of Losing a Customer

Did you know that 68 percent of customers are lost because an employee didn't handle their complaint well? The percentage is staggering but true! *U.S. News and World Report* found that:

- 1 percent of customers leave because someone in the company dies.
- 3 percent change location.
- 5 percent make other friendships.
- 9 percent go to competition.
- 14 percent are dissatisfied.
- 68 percent leave because of indifference by one employee!

It gets worse! Research shows that, out of 25 dissatisfied customers:

- Only one customer complains.
- Twenty-four are dissatisfied but don't complain.
- Six of the 24 noncomplainers have "serious" problems.

The 24 noncomplainers tell between 10 and 20 other people about their bad experience. From a pool of 25 customers, therefore, between 250 and 500 potential customers learn about the bad service.

These percentages work in exactly the same way on a personal level! If you are grumpy and unhelpful, most people will not confront you face-to-face. They'll simply tell other people about you, and pretty soon you're left wondering why no one asks you out to lunch.

Here's an example of how easy it is to lose a customer. We have worked with Motorola for over two decades; they are among our best customers. Some years ago, we got so much work from them that we became tired and irritable. We were scripting satellite broadcasts, writing training manuals, facilitating workshops, conducting pilot programs, producing videos, and doing much more.

To cover our growing workload, instead of hiring more staff (which is what Motorola assumed), we simply became overworked. We made mistakes, and that wasn't all. Because we had worked and partnered with Motorola for so long, we felt we had earned the right to complain. So we did!

One of the Motorola people with whom we were on friendly terms gave us fair warning. We were at lunch one day when the manager said, "I have to tell you that my people are looking at other vendors. They make their own decisions about who they work with and some companies cost less than you." Then the manager said bluntly, "If you don't change the way you do business, we may not be doing business with you anymore!"

Unbelievably, we still didn't listen. We felt so much a part of our customer Motorola that we considered ourselves bulletproof and, like lemmings, we jumped to our doom. Shortly after the warning, we handed a participant guide to one of their project managers. After finding some typos, the manager looked up and said, "So you haven't run it through spell-check yet?" That was the day we lost our edge.

Finally, work from Motorola trickled to nothing and we got what we asked for—peace and quiet! We lost our best customer. Over the next year, our revenues dropped by 40 percent, and it almost cost us our business. It took another two years to find our competitive edge, bring Motorola back, and develop a bigger, more diverse customer base. It was an expensive lesson, but one we will never forget. Thank you, Motorola!

Maybe you are thinking that one lost customer will not have the same effect on you, because you don't have your own company. Wrong! Everything you do has a direct impact on your life.

Here's a positive story about a person who delivered Domino's Pizzas. The delivery person was in a hotel elevator delivering pizzas to the 15th floor, sharing the elevator with two other people. The three started talking and even got out at the same floor. A few minutes later, one of the people began speaking to the pizza delivery person.

Guest: "How come you're delivering pizza? With your personality you should be a salesperson."

Delivery person:	"This is my last week. I've just started working for a training company selling their programs."
Guest:	"What kind of programs?"
Delivery person:	"Selling skills, customer service, negotiating—they create a lot of different programs."
Guest:	"We're looking for training in customer care right now. I would be interested to hear more about your programs. Here's my card."

The delivery person is now one of our top salespeople, and we've been doing business with the client he met in the elevator for three years. The point is that you never know who is a potential customer and how easy it is either to win or to lose a customer.

Take a look at Scandinavian Airline Systems (SAS). In 1981, SAS had done so poorly, it lost $8 million. Jan Carlzon, the president, researched the problem and found the lost revenues had nothing to do with airplanes, hangars, or standard operating procedures. Instead, he found that SAS was losing money because customers were unhappy!

Research showed that every time a customer comes into contact with an employee (baggage handling, flight reservations, etc.), the customer forms an opinion of the airline. Carlzon defined these experiences as "moments of truth." He calculated that every SAS customer has five "moments of truth" on each flight. Ten million customers represent 50 million opportunities to form a good or bad opinion of SAS! Carlzon decided that SAS needed to focus on customer care, and guess what? A little over one year later, the company turned an $8 million loss into a $71 million gross profit!

How did they do it?

- Managers served the frontline service providers so that they in turn could serve the passengers.
- Catering staff kept planes well stocked, so that flight attendants could assist passengers.
- Maintenance workers made it possible for flights to take off on time.

It seems almost too simple, doesn't it? Yet it's so obvious that major corporations often forget to do it. They don't focus on the customer's "moments of truth." In fact, a friend of ours whose father was a maintenance worker for a large airline said they used to joke that "the gate should be renamed 'final assembly'!" Not the kind of comment that a customer would like to hear, is it?

How to Calculate Your Moments of Truth

This exercise will help you determine how many "moments of truth" you have with your customers each day.

MOMENTS OF TRUTH

- Take your mind back to yesterday at the very beginning of the morning.
- Make a check mark in the space below for every time you communicated with a customer.

_____

_____

_____

_____

_____

_____

_____

_____

_____

_____

_____

_____

_____

- Count up your checkmarks

These are your moments of truth: opportunities to satisfy and retain existing customers, to interact with colleagues in a helpful manner, to build teams, and to manage people better.

Now recall the type of interactions you had. Close your eyes for a moment and remember your customers' faces, body language, and tone of voice. How did the interactions go?

SUPER SERVICE SELF-ASSESSMENT TOOL

Circle five words that most clearly show how you feel about your customers:

a. Interested	Empathetic	Informed
b. Problems	Issues	Jargon
c. Thanks	Clarity	Acknowledged
d. Ignored	Disinterested	Unclear
e. Green	Pleasant	Content
f. Disturbed	Red	Unpleasant

SUPER SERVICE SELF-ASSESSMENT RESULTS

1. Each row has a letter beside it.
2. Write down the letters that correspond to each of your circled words.

   _____

3. If three words or more appear on lines a, c, or e, *you enjoy interacting with your customers.*
4. If three words or more appear on lines b, d, or f, *you do not enjoy interacting with your customers.*

Don't worry about your scores too much at this point. You would not be reading *Super Service* if you didn't want to make some changes. The first step toward any kind of change is awareness. Congratulations! You have just made the first step.

Connecting Heart and Soul

Connecting with a customer's heart and soul means experiencing your customers as fully rounded human beings with all the joy, family issues, money scares, and work problems that every one of us experiences from time to time.

To connect with a customer "heart and soul" takes no more than standing in front of a mirror and looking at yourself. Do it! Go to a mirror, and you will see before you a customer! How does it feel? How do you act as a customer? If you have an argument with your beloved, do you allow it to ring in your ears all day? Or do you still manage to behave as a great customer?

Chances are that, if you aren't a great customer, it will be a push for you to give *Super Service*. Try the following exercise:

- Take a moment to sit quietly and relax.
- Inhale one deep breath.
- Hold it.
- Ask yourself, "Do I treat my customers as I like to be treated?"
- Exhale.

Every person is a customer at some time or another. Put yourself into your customer's frame of mind. How do you as a customer like to be treated? To help you gauge your attitude, complete the special checklist on the next page.

HOW YOU FEEL ABOUT YOUR CUSTOMERS

Read this checklist and circle your answers as "T" (true) or "F" (false):

1. T F Customers want too much service.

2. T F Customers need to understand my side of the story.

3. T F Customers should not expect a fast response.

4. T F Customers complain about insignificant problems.

5. T F Placing a customer on hold for two minutes is okay.

6. T F Telling the customer I handle lots of issues is okay.

7. T F I need some appreciation from customers.

8. T F Someone else should deal with irate customers.

ANSWERS

The answers are written as if you are the customer. This way you will understand the point of view from a customer perspective.

1. FALSE   Customers want too much service.

As a customer yourself, you want and expect good service; there's no such thing as too much.

2. FALSE   Customers need to understand my side of the story.

You are concerned with your own problems, especially if the service provider is responsible for them. You are not interested in their side of the story.

3. FALSE   Customers should not expect a fast response.

As a customer, you may have tried to solve the problem yourself. By the time you've called the service provider, you've already spent too much time on it and you expect a fast response.

4. FALSE   Customers complain about insignificant problems.

*No problem is too small to a customer. If you have a problem and the service provider tells you it's insignificant, how does that make **you** feel? Very frustrated!*

5. FALSE   Placing a customer on hold for two minutes is okay.

Close your eyes and get someone to tell you when a minute is up! What were you thinking and feeling as the time went on? Putting anyone on hold for longer than 30 seconds may lead to damaging thoughts.

6. FALSE   Telling the customer I handle lots of issues is okay.

As a customer, I interpret this to mean that the product or service is prone to lots of problems. Not good for long-term business!

7. FALSE   I need some appreciation from customers.

What goes around comes around, and we all like appreciation. Often that appreciation comes from a different source. Customers are not always appreciative, even of good service; they expect it!

8. FALSE   Someone else should deal with irate customers.

Have you ever been an irate customer? If so, you probably know that you are usually annoyed at the product or the company, not the person serving you. But if that person starts to take it personally, you feel the tension build. So, from either point of view, don't take things personally.

Positive Energy

Julia works for a large store and is one of their top salespeople. Why? Julia loves people. Walk into the place and she smiles just because you've walked in. It's not a "fake" smile, either—she is a "Marty, high-five" kind of person. People want her to serve them. She raises the pleasure level of buying just by showing the delight that you've walked into the store. Whether you are a new customer or a regular, Julia has the same high level of energy.

Also, Julia knows the product. She makes practical suggestions. Of course, we buy more than we went in for, but it's so much fun, it's okay! We don't even get the usual buyer's remorse.

Julia connects heart and soul with her customers. She has the desire to serve: "Oh I'm so glad you came in. I've missed you! It's so good to see you!" Okay, on the printed page the reaction may sound like too much, but with the brightness and the smile it's a winner.

And who benefits? Everyone! The store, the customer, and, of course, Julia. She enjoys her job, and she does it well. She's acknowledged by her colleagues, she's on first-name terms with top management, and she's rewarded monetarily: Julia has been promoted and given a raise!

Can everyone do it the way she does? No. We may not have her particular brand of charisma! What will work just as well is a willingness to serve and be served. Have you ever been in your local food store and stood at the checkout? Are you a great customer? Do you ask the clerk if he or she is having a good day? Does the clerk need a smile? Just like Marty at his job, the clerk can stand there or just *stand there*!

Consider Jim. Before he understood the "what-goes-around-comes-around" principle, he was a rotten customer and a rotten server. He demanded things as a customer, and gave little as a server. So what did he get in return? Demands and little else! He was treated with horror and fear. Did he get what he wanted? Usually not. When he did, it never felt right. Jim lived in a war zone. Then he went to a training workshop and had a breakthrough! To be great at *Super Service, even when he didn't feel like it and even when customers didn't deserve it*, he had to be a great customer himself.

Jim learned that we all serve and are served every day of our lives, that our attitude is the important part. Much of our lives is determined by the tone of the script we write for ourselves: We can choose comedy, drama, tragedy, or romance. It's our choice!

Super Service Workouts

Below are some *Super Service* affirmations. Pick one to use each day.

SUPER SERVICE AFFIRMATIONS

1. My *customer is anyone who isn't me*.
2. My customers are people first.
3. I am a great customer.
4. I take full responsibility for solving customer problems.
5. I keep all the promises I make to my customers.
6. I establish and maintain good rapport with customers.
7. I respect my customer's point of view.
8. I listen to understand how my customers feel.
9. I look beyond their words to understand their feelings.
10. I always acknowledge what my customers are feeling.
11. I show a desire to serve.
12. I smile and maintain eye contact.
13. I sit straight and I stand straight.
14. I will not "give away the shop" to bribe customers.
15. I realize that every interaction is a positive attitude opportunity.
16. I control my biases and my judgments.
17. I show my customers that I care and I am on their side.
18. I acknowledge my customers' priorities.
19. I take responsibility and use "I" instead of "we."
20. I connect with my customers' "heart and soul."

CHECK-IN

You know who your external customers are, but do you know your internal customers and how your job affects theirs? Make a list of the internal customers that your job most affects: include the boss, colleagues, peers, assistants, different departments or locations. Use the example as a guideline.

Internal Customers	How My Job Affects Theirs
Michelle Somers	*Updating address and phone info*

ACTION: HOW AM I DOING?

Read the following statements and circle "Yes" or "No" as applicable.

Yes　No　I show a desire to serve.

Yes　No　I am a problem solver.

Yes　No　I recently helped solve a difficult problem.

Yes　No　I gather information well.

Yes　No　People understand the information I give.

Yes　No　I check for understanding.

Yes　No　People feel comfortable asking me for help.

Yes　No　I am a considerate customer.

Yes　No　I give more than I take.

Yes　No　I would enjoy being served by someone like me.

ACTION: HOW AM I DOING? RESPONSE

- Go to the above exercise and count up the number of "Yes" responses and the number of "No" responses.
- If you had six or more "Yes" responses, you are already understanding what *Super Service* is all about.
- If you had six or more "No" responses, you could improve in some areas. Use the space below to write one main area for improvement:

- My main area for improvement is _____

- I will improve this today by _____

Chapter 2

Serving Up Your Best
(Even When Feeling Your Worst)

To serve others is ultimately to serve ourselves because when
we open our hearts, our spirit grows and becomes stronger.

Here is how two of our clients, who participated in our *Super Service* workshop, answered the following three questions:

Kathy—DeVry University, Dean of Student Affairs
1. **As a customer, what do you want?**
   "I want to be given full attention, smiled at, heard, and taken care of as soon as possible. I want to know if there are delays, why and when to expect delivery."

2. **As a customer, what do you feel stops you from getting what you want?**
   "Usually, it is when the staff does not take ownership or responsibility. They see you as an interruption and hide behind 'the System' to do the bare minimum of work."

3. **In your experience, what do customer service people do best?**
   "By far, they take ownership and stay with you until they know you are satisfied or a decision is final. They remain positive with you even if they cannot do what you want, but they let you know why and what can be done."

Lena—Southwest Carpenter Training Fund
1. **As a customer, what do you want?**
   "I want someone who smiles and says, 'How are you doing today? What can I help you with?'"

2. **As a customer, what do you feel stops you from getting what you want?**
   "When someone has an attitude and looks like he doesn't want to be doing this job."

3. **In your experience, what do customer service people do best?**
   "Customer service people do their best when they are happy and love what they are doing."

Let me tell you a story about Jeff. A few years ago, Jeff's dad was very ill with cancer, so ill that we all knew he was going to die. Jeff and his dad loved each other, but they weren't close in the "come here and give me a hug" kind of way. In fact, his dad had never said outright, "I love you." And Jeff had always felt that they needed to say this to each other. It wasn't that his dad didn't love him; it was that he was worried about him.

So Jeff flew to Newcastle-upon-Tyne, in England, to visit his dad in the hospital. When he came back home he said, "I had the best visit with my dad." I asked him what happened and he said, "I told him that I loved him, and he said, 'I love you too.' He said he was really proud of me and thought I had made a good life for myself and my family. We reminisced about his time during the war and how difficult it had been, and how when he was a salesman and had to travel away, how hard it had been not seeing the family. My dad is an amazing man."

"Does he know he's going to die?" I asked.

"Oh yes. In fact, he's refusing any more treatment. He just wants to go home and die in his own bed." Jeff looked down for a moment, "I don't think he's going to last much longer. But he told me to come back home . . . that he was glad we'd talked and now he was ready to die."

▼ KEY POINT

Super Service is about living your life in a certain way at work and at home. It is about being open to communication on every level. Don't wait a moment longer—pick up the telephone and tell your loved one, "I love you!"

The next day, Jeff was giving a large *Super Service* keynote talk for 1,000+ people, and I was along to assist. Just before he was due to go on stage, Jeff's cell phone rang. It was his mom. I heard the silence on the cell phone and knew something bad had happened. Jeff spoke reassuring words of comfort to her, listened, and told her he would see her very soon. Then, he put the cell phone down and told me his dad had passed away the night before. It's strange, but when someone dies after a long illness there is almost a sense of relief that it has finally happened; but then there is a big sadness because even though the death was expected, the fact is we will never see that person again.

"What do you want to do?" I asked him, thinking that he would not want to continue; after all a keynote talk is all about emphasizing key points in an entertaining, upbeat way.

"I go on! They're expecting me."

"But they'll understand, if you don't . . ."

"We won't say a word."

So off he went and did one of the best keynote speeches of his life. Of course, he couldn't really cancel because . . . well I guess it's like the actors say, *the show must go on.*

And that's what giving *Super Service* is all about. It doesn't matter what is happening in our personal lives. If we have a commitment to be somewhere, and people are depending on us, we have to do it.

> ▼
>
> ## Key Point
>
> Keep your commitments. You will feel good about yourself and others will appreciate you even more.

The point of this story is that it's about doing what you have to do, no matter what your condition is. If you are sick, be the best you can in spite of this. If you are bored, have a great attitude anyway.

Now I'm not saying you have to go to work when you are sick, or never take time off when someone close to you dies. What I am saying is this: Go to work and be great. If something happens in your personal life, leave it at home. Because here's the thing, when you go to work and have a great attitude—no matter what is going on—great, amazing things happen. For Jeff, he got to feel his father's pride. He told me later, "I knew that my dad was with me that morning. And I knew he was proud of me. It's what he always wanted me to do—to do a good job, so that's what I did."

> ▼
>
> ## Key Point
>
> Always do the best job that you can do. You'll feel great as a result.

Pushing through and doing the job no matter what is going on, mentally or physically, reaps its own fantastic rewards. At work, at home, at play, be the best.

You see, sadness, unhappiness, anger, upset, and depression are all thoughts that keep us down. They keep us staying in bed. They keep us feeling bad. They make us feel indifferent to our customers.

It is impossible to create a happy life if we allow "bad" events or situations to take all of the focus. Yes, Jeff could have cancelled and gone home and been upset about his dad's death, but what would that have done? Nothing really. The event planners would have created something else; they would have found someone to fill in for Jeff.

When something bad happens in your life, does it make you feel bad? Do you start to act in a certain way? When something bad happens, how do you choose to react? Because the wonderful things about being human are that we have a brain and we can choose to react in whichever way we want.

▼

Key Point

It is your choice on what you focus on in your life. If you focus on bad things—that is what you will see. If you focus on good things—that is what you will see. Decide when you wake up in the morning: "What do I want to focus on today?"

Focus on the Customer

When you feel great, serving is fairly easy, but it's very difficult when you feel depressed or have major problems in your life. Fortunately, showing a desire to serve is a skill that can be learned, no matter how bad you are feeling.

What if you believe that showing the desire to serve means becoming a doormat? All others want to wipe their feet on you: Get me that! Bring me this! Do it now!

In truth, the opposite happens. Serving takes great courage, power, leadership, and a strong spirit. To serve others is ultimately to serve ourselves because, when we open our hearts, our spirit grows and becomes stronger. Here's how you do it:

1. Put your own feelings backstage for a short while.
2. Focus on the customer.
3. Bring the customer to front stage in your mind.
4. Take care of the customer's needs.

Think of the great courage it takes to serve. Think of anyone in the public eye: presidents, first ladies, kings, queens, supermodels, Grammy award winners, and so on. Public figures, as humans, experience illness, family crisis, and events outside their control. Yet, unlike lesser-known people, the ones who live in the public eye have lives that are arranged sometimes years in advance. They can't cancel (and if they do, they soon get a bad reputation). They have to put on a smile and move through the pain. It takes lots of power and leadership to do that. It's much easier to stay home in bed.

Just as leaders decide they have the strength to serve, so can you. The strength comes from the thought that, "I am here to help my customers. What do they want? How can I help them?"

When we as human beings become servers, we become the most precious people in the world. We become conscious of other people and look for opportunities to help, instead of worrying so much about our own problems. If you have ever helped anyone in this way, you know how uplifted you feel.

You may have heard the saying, "Let go, let flow." That's all you have to do to feel your best. Let your mind be free of all the chatter. Let go of all of your problems, worries, and ego, and let your mind become nothing so that you can be everything for your customers.

When you are being your best, you feel in alignment with all that is good about your life. You are in touch with an inner strength that enables you to turn off the little voice in your head that says you aren't good enough, or thin enough, or fit enough, or good-looking enough, or smart enough, or wealthy enough, or "enough" of anything!

Being your best means accepting yourself as you are right now! It means that you wouldn't change a thing. Sometimes, when we look back at our lives, we remember the things we did or didn't do, things that, with our current wisdom, we think we could have done better. Because we are older and wiser, we think, "What a mess I made of my life!" If only I had studied more, had different friends, had a better family, and so on.

You can change this way of thinking by repeating the following phrase: "I am the best, and I'm getting better and better every day!" It almost sounds simple, but sometimes the simplest things are the most effective.

You may be thinking, "I have a life, I don't want to bring my customer to front stage and put myself backstage!" Yes, it's true, you do have a life. If part of your life includes working with customers, why not accept it? When you do, magical things happen and your own life becomes much easier. And if you don't want to be serving customers, then be great in your job right now, and work toward becoming a line-manager or maybe a career where you don't interact so much with people.

It's like this: Water is wet, rocks are hard, and customers want to be served. Depending on your job, you call customers by different names: fans, constituents, loyal subjects, clients, patients, etc. They all expect service, so why not serve them? Make it easier for you to help them; get into the flow of delivering *Super Service* and discover how fresh it feels to do a great job! All we suggest is this: If your job is to serve customers, maybe you can empty your mind of some of your own things and leave a little space for them.

HOW TO SHOW A DESIRE TO SERVE

1. **Be in control of your attitude.**
   If you wake up with a bad attitude or something triggers it during the day, become an actor for a while. Think of a person who has a positive attitude. See him or her in your mind. Imagine how the person sits, stands, walks, and talks. Feel yourself become like that person.

2. **Let your anger go.**
   Anger is poisonous and feeds on itself. If anger comes up, simply take a deep breath, hold it for a count of three, and then let it go. Feel the anger release with the breath. We breathe not just to bring in oxygen, but to release carbon dioxide. Let your anger go when you exhale.

3. **Maintain a positive attitude.**
   If you want to feel satisfied in your job and experience energy and fulfillment at the end of your day, have a positive attitude. Think good thoughts. Do the right thing. Make the best choices.

4. **Affirm your day.**
   When you wake up in the morning, brush your teeth, look at yourself in the mirror, and say out loud, "Today is going to be a great day. No matter what I am doing, I am going to do it with the desire to serve. I will be positive, upbeat, and ready to be the best for my customer!"

Step Outside Yourself

By serving only the "worthy" customers, you shut out the majority of people. Let's face it: Most people are not like us. They don't look like us or act like us. If we were all the same, there wouldn't be newspapers, or books, or articles, or TV programs, or movies.

In Victorian times, we used to have the "deserving" poor. These were the people who had no money, but still swept their mud floor and kept themselves as clean as possible. The "deserving" poor got help from charities. The "undeserving" poor were the dirty, unkempt people who didn't look as though they deserved help. Every time we treat customers in a lessened way, because we feel they are "undeserving," we step backward. We need to step forward. Be at your best by celebrating the differences, and enjoying the interesting and different styles of people. Show a desire to serve everyone with equal skill and wisdom.

Most of the time, we are too busy in our own little worlds to really see the people around us. We meet people for the first time, and after a couple of seconds we have categorized, labeled, and placed them in a box. Some people get put in boxes never to be seen again, and these people could be your best allies in the customer care cycle.

We might prefer to rub elbows with people who look smart and wear the right clothes, but they may also be too busy to help us in a crisis with a customer. If we can just stop our judgments about people—let them be our teachers, accept them for the wonderful people they are, with all their quirks and strange little habits (because, of course, we don't have any)—we would be more than halfway to providing *Super Service*.

On the coming pages are affirmations and exercises that may help you to step outside yourself and find a role model, a teacher, or a mentor.

SUPER SERVICE AFFIRMATIONS

1. *Everyone is my teacher.*
2. I am in touch with my feelings and can relate them to others.
3. I learn from everyone around me.
4. I am awake and help others to awaken.
5. I am objective about people.
6. I am open to every different kind of person.
7. I see the potential in everyone.
8. I let go of my fear about people and accept them all as they are.
9. I look to a mentor as a wise and trusted counselor.
10. I value serving others.

Take Responsibility for Your Mistakes

We were having a plumber do some work. He was supposed to have the job finished by the time we came back from a short business trip. We explained that we would be returning with a visitor, so the bathroom had to be finished.

Of course, it wasn't done. The bathroom was all ripped apart. The tiling was uneven and a single pipe was sticking out of the wall. Plaster lay in the bath and on the floor. It was a mess!

The plumber gave us a long story about a bad tooth with a complicated sinus infection that led him to the hospital. His head was hung, and his eyes flitted right and left like a pendulum. He didn't sound or look as though he was telling the truth.

Plumber: "How was your trip?" he asked in an attempt to divert the attention from him. Needless to say, it did not work.

Gees: "When can you finish it?" we asked.

Plumber: "Probably Thursday."

Gees: "Thursday! Definitely?"

Plumber: "Yes!" he said.

He finished the main part of the job on the Friday, and finished off other things during the next few weeks.

Will we ever use him again? No! Does it matter to him? Yes! He certainly won't get a good reference from us, and we will call the company that referred him and tell them what happened. More importantly, he did not feel good about himself.

If we cannot look our fellow human beings in the eye and maintain a clear and steady gaze, there is something wrong! If we do not feel that we did a good job, then we need to accept responsibility for that. Here are a few simple things that can help you take responsibility:

HOW TO TAKE RESPONSIBILITY

1. **Make "I" statements.**
    "I will call the service department."
    "I will look into that and get back to you by next Monday."
2. **Complete things.**
    Make a list of things you need to complete. It could be as simple as writing to a friend or a parent. Then get those things done!
3. **Take notes.**
    If you don't write down what you said you will do, it may never happen.
4. **Keep your word.**
    If you have ever been stood up or had someone change plans on you at the last minute, you know how bad it feels. Keep your word, and people will keep their word with you.

Super Service is about you. How you treat people is how others will treat you. If you take time and care with people, they will take time and care with you. *Super Service* does not mean that you are doing everything with an ulterior motive; it does not mean that if you do something for someone, you expect it back threefold. It may never come from the person you expect it to come from, but it will come.

ACTION

Next time you are with a customer (either internal or external), evaluate yourself on how you are doing. Here is a very short list of questions to answer:

1. Was I honest?
2. Did I complete the task?
3. Did I help the situation?
4. Did I show a desire to serve?

Super Service is about you caring about you. It's about you feeling good at the end of the day. You can start right now, today. Keep an eye on yourself by asking, "Am I conscious of what I am saying, what I am doing, and how I am doing it?"

ACTION

To live an amazing life; here are four key things to do every day:

1. Every morning, decide what you want to focus on for the day—good or bad? "Today I will focus on the good."
2. When something bad happens, as far as possible, keep your commitments; do not let the bad event overwhelm you and take over your life.
3. When something good happens, enjoy it; relish the good things in your life and rejoice in them.
4. Be thankful; give thanks for what happens in your life; thank yourself, thank others, and have an attitude of thankfulness.

Super Service is about you taking ownership of your life. When you understand that you are not responsible for everything that happens, but you are responsible for how you react and what you choose to focus on, you are putting yourself in the power seat! You are in charge.

PART II

Seven Keys to
Delivering Super Service

Chapter 3

CUSTOMER SERVICE KEY 1

The Right Attitude

Seeing the good in yourself and your circumstances
is an important step in having a positive attitude.

Here is how two of our clients, who participated in our *Super Service* workshop, answered the following three questions:

Amr. F.—HSBC Bank, *Customer Service Representative*

1. **As a customer, what do you want?**

   "Attitude, quality, and service. And if you are asking yourself why service is last it is because the first thing that the customer feels is attitude from the one providing the service. The customer then looks for quality, which gives a good or bad impression about the company or bank, and finally, how the employee serves. If I was to give a percentage I would say:

   - **Attitude—**25%
   - **Quality—**25%
   - **Service—**50%"

2. **As a customer, what do you feel stops you from getting what you want?**

   "Attitude, quality, and service. If the attitude and quality are lacking, for sure the service will be in the low ranking, because as I said in the first place, those **three words** *are related to each other."*

3. **In your experience, what do customer service people do best?**

   "Attitude, quality, and service."

Joseph—Trendl Associates, Ltd., *President & CEO*

1. **As a customer, what do you want?**

   "I want to feel good about spending my money."

2. **As a customer, what do you feel stops you from getting what you want?**

   "People who don't care about my experience. They simply want to ring up the sale and move on to some personal business that I've interrupted trying to make my purchase."

3. **In your experience, what do customer service people do best?**

   "I have so few examples of what they do best that I cannot answer."

Thank You for Your Business

My daughter and I were taking an evening walk the other night through the streets of Chicago, when we came upon a "diving shop." I passed my scuba diving certification many years ago when I lived in Scotland. The problem is that most international diving places need a PADI certification; my Scottish certificate doesn't count. So I said, "You know I've been meaning to get my PADI certification for ages, maybe I'll sign up, and take it here." So we went in.

Immediately, we got the sense of "busyness." There were two store assistants. One was serving a customer and the other store assistant was busy—I don't know what she was doing exactly—stocking shelves, undoing boxes of inventory; something that was making her grumpy, and seeming to be in the middle of a big mess on the floor. So we kind of lingered a while . . . looking at the shelves, the merchandise, the walls, the floor, the ceiling. Then, finally, she looked up and my daughter asked, "Is there an inside pool?"

The store assistant answered in a gruff tone, "Over there . . . ," shrugged her shoulders toward a door that must have led to a basement, and then carried on doing whatever it was that she was doing. My daughter and I looked at each other and then, without another word, we left the store.

"Boy, oh boy!"

We looked at each other and carried on walking down the street.

"I was going to book up some lessons for PADI!" I said. "They've just lost my business."

"I know . . . it's crazy!"

And it is crazy, but mostly it's really sad. Because somewhere there is a store owner who has gone to the trouble of renting a store, purchasing merchandise, building an indoor swimming pool, hiring staff . . . and all the other hundreds of things that need to be done to open a diving store. Yet, because of the bad attitude of the people in the store, two prospective customers have just walked out! The attitude of the two store assistants said, "Go away! We don't want to be bothered with you . . . we're too busy 'doing' our job!"

The only reason a store exists is to get customers, and they had us actually in the store, and yet we walked out. What could they have done differently? The answer is simple, either one of the assistants could have looked up when we walked in, made eye contact, smiled, and said, "Thank you for coming into our store this evening, I'll be with you in just a moment." Or, "Welcome to our diving shop, please take a look around, we have our own indoor swimming pool and I'll be happy to show you it in a moment."

▼

KEY POINT

Attitude is what counts more than anything else when you are providing customer service. It only takes a moment to make eye contact, smile, say, "welcome . . ." and gain a customer. It only takes a moment to not bother, and to lose a customer.

Here is an example of great customer service. We went into Home Depot to look for some enamel paint to touch up a small dent on our white stove. We walked in and went to the aisle that said *Paint.* Then we looked up and down the aisle searching for the specific paint. Finally, we found the type of paint we wanted but not the right color. Just then, a store assistant came up and said, "Can I help you?" We explained what we were looking for, and he started to look too. We were almost about to give up, when he said, "I know we have it somewhere around here." Then he looked on another shelf and there it was. Then he went on to explain how to use it. "Just put a very thin layer on . . . let it dry and keep applying it until it is even with the enamel on your stove."

It was a small thing, and the store didn't make much money on that particular item, but we keep going back there, because we have never had a bad experience with their staff. People go out of their way to find things, to walk us over to the aisle, to check that we are being helped. They're just fantastic! And I've noticed also that people do say "Welcome" when we walk in, or "How are you doing today?"

That's what customer service is about—taking care of the customer. The customer has money and a need to purchase or they would not be in the store. The customer service provider's job is to be excellent with the customer: to provide *Super Service,* eye contact, a smile, and a welcoming attitude.

▼

Key Point

Customers make the world go around. When a customer comes into your space, whether it is face-to-face, over the telephone, or via the Internet . . . your job is to make them feel welcome. It only takes a moment—so make that moment count in a positive way.

There are seven basic keys to delivering great customer service. Together, these keys form a flow of communication between you and your customer. Keeping this flow smooth will help you and your customer by lessening the conflicts and anxiety caused by miscommunication. When you are "in the flow," your job will run more smoothly and you will find it more enjoyable.

Getting into the flow always begins with *Customer Service Key 1: Have the Right Attitude.* Whether you are reaching agreement, checking understanding, or taking action, having the right attitude is always the first and most important key to *Super Service.*

The easiest way to show the importance of this first key is to give you an example of someone who did *not* have it:

Both Jeff and I have held a life insurance policy for over 10 years with one insurance agent. We never hear from John unless the rates change. Recently, he sent literature that caused us to look at buying a 20-year fixed-rate policy from him. Over the course of a week, our agent spoke to each of us at separate times, so we both received slightly different information.

When we had time to sit down and look at the two policies, we saw that we'd be paying an extra $500 for the first year. When we called to ask him about it, he didn't want to listen. This is how it went:

Gees: "John, we noticed that we will be paying $500 more for the first year."

John: "Have you done your blood test to qualify you for the new policy yet?" he replied, ignoring the question.

Gees: "Not yet. What about the premium?"

John: "The blood test has to be done by next week," he continued, still ignoring the question.

Gees: "What about the premium?"

John: "We already discussed it."

Gees: "Not with me!"

John: "I discussed it with your partner," he replied gruffly. "If you don't get your blood work done soon, you will miss the window of opportunity!"

John failed to keep our trust by not having the right attitude. He didn't answer our questions and he used manipulative tactics to get us to buy a different policy. Well, guess what? We ended up wanting to miss the window and, to cut a long story short, we no longer felt loyalty to this agent. We looked for another policy with a different agent and will definitely not recommend John to anyone else.

You might think you have to do lots of things to get the right attitude. But the strange thing about having and maintaining the right attitude is that it starts with *taking away*, not *adding to*.

Next time you are with a customer (either internal or external), empty your mind of everything except that person. Stop your thoughts and allow yourself to be in the same space with them. Stop thinking about your next task or your project deadline. Allow yourself to become still, just for a moment or two, and let the frenzy of your world continue without you. This is the "taking away" process; you "take away" all distractions.

When we listen to our "internal dialogue" instead of to the person who is talking, we might as well be at home sleeping, because we are certainly not there for them. We want them to talk faster, so that we can get on with the important stuff—which usually translates to *our* stuff. We hate the joke, or the story that we heard last week, or even the week before. We don't have time to listen to them about their children, spouse, finances, or health problems. "We have 'real' work to do, for goodness sake!"

If you are in the business of customers, if you work with people, if people are in your life, you need to take the time to listen—with a positive attitude. You need to empty yourselves of your own immediate concerns and focus your complete attention on serving your customers.

There's a diner near where we live, and whoever walks through the door, the owner always greets them with a big, "Welcome, sit wherever you like!" We always feel welcome so we go there quite often, and we have a lot of choices living in Chicago! Making customers feel welcome is key to success, and it's not just face-to-face in small diners where it matters.

I just read about a care director who went to work for a national cellular network with a very large call center. From his experience he knew that customer service, rather than price and product, would be their long-term source of market differentiation—

mobile phones were about lifestyle management for people on the move. But upper management did not share his vision. They decided, "We don't want a relationship with customers. Customers are a pain in the rear; they just cost us money when they call us."

He was told that customer care is a cost center, and his job was "to reduce the cost as much as possible." At that point, he knew he was in the wrong organization and soon left to pursue a path of helping organizations who do "get" customers, to become more customer-centric. Over the intervening years, his former employer gradually slipped from No. 1 to fourth out of four!

From small, to medium to large—it doesn't matter what size the company is—customers are individuals—they want to be treated as such.

Maintain a Positive Frame of Mind

We were sitting at a sidewalk cafe when an elderly man nodded toward our table and asked, "Are we all happy?"

"Yes," we chorused. He smiled and walked on. We recognized him as W. Clement Stone, one of the founders of Positive Mental Attitude. He was probably a millionaire many times over, yet this elderly man, who died in 2002, still took the time to ask a bunch of strangers if we were all happy!

There was no reason for him to bother about us. We weren't customers, friends, or even neighbors. There was nothing visible in it for him except that he was obviously bright and alert to everything going on around him. He made the choice to be happy, and it touched everyone around him.

Most of us tend to think happiness is elusive—something we've left behind or something we are working toward. But happiness is *right now*. Happiness is waking up to a dark cloud-filled sky and going on the picnic anyway.

Let's say you have a lousy job. You are underpaid. Your colleagues are different or even seem strange to you. You have to work an 11-hour day. The person at the next workstation is a grouch. Your boss hates you. No one asks you to lunch. The customers are all demanding. The product is terrible. You don't have a corner office. You do have a corner office and you feel left out. The elevator takes hours, and on and on.

You may think, how can I possibly be happy? If I look at my life realistically, I will probably shoot myself in the foot just to get sick leave! There is no way I can have a positive frame of mind. I would be mad to enjoy this situation.

The reality, however, is very different. You have a job! Hallelujah! In a world where poverty and famine are a constant, having a job is a real bonus. You still hate it? Then work like crazy to get another one. Still do your work, be the best you can be, and look for another job. Get a great resume together. Hunt the online job sites and the newspapers. Ask friends. Get a headhunter. Go to a career counselor. Make your focus a new job.

Then understand one thing: You will have equally annoying people and situations in your new job. Why? Because until you see how good you are, you will not recognize the hidden good in other people. Seeing the good in you is an important step toward having a positive attitude.

Once, during a sermon about happiness, the speaker had some great tips and introduced them all with such phrases as, "This may sound dumb but . . ." or "I know this seems crazy . . ."

Why? Why do we think it's crazy to smile even though we feel like crying? Or to read an uplifting book, or listen to wonderful music, or do any of the things we can do to raise our spirit?

Having a positive frame of mind is hard only if we want it to be hard. If having a hard life is easier to us, then we will interpret having a positive frame of mind as being harder, because that's the way we want it to be!

"But I'm not a happy and outgoing person," you say? Not so. We all have the potential to be whoever we want to be. All it takes is a little positive energy. Instead of being a drain, decide to be a filler-up. Tell yourself, "I will fill my life with joy. I will give. I will serve. I will do whatever is necessary to get the job done."

Our training and consulting business demands a lot of airline travel. The best airline we have ever used is Singapore Airlines because the employees go beyond their duty. They actively look for problems and often see them before they even arise: parents with children needing extra hands, frail people with heavy luggage, nervous first-timers who don't see their seat numbers. It's wonderful to experience people who have this desire to serve.

If we didn't have so many frequent-flyer miles racked up with the airline we usually fly with, we wouldn't use them because we are treated like cattle. One time we saw two parents way ahead of us, boarding the flight with their three young children, two strollers, and one set of luggage wheels. The mom went first with a child and a stroller. The dad struggled with the rest. The flight attendant simply stood there and told him where he *could not* put his stroller or luggage wheels. The flight attendant was obviously very angry at the passenger for being a parent and having baby gear to be stowed away. This irritated the father, set the children off, and got all the surrounding passengers in a tizzy, as some sided with him and others with the flight attendant. As the flight was being attended to in the cockpit, there was chaos back in the "people pit."

We wondered how Singapore Airlines flight attendants would prepare for their day. Maybe something like this:

1. **Prepare yourself.** Before the passengers come on board, prepare yourself for every event.
2. **Think about why you are here.** Look for opportunities to help.
3. **Pay attention.** Look for people in need: elderly, parents with young children, people with physical disabilities, and nervous first-timers.
4. **Maintain a positive frame of mind.** Look for ways to make a positive difference.

This is about you. How you feel at the end of the day is determined by keeping a positive attitude through the rough times. The only way you can do that is to be the best you can be, not to take things personally, and keep smiling.

Even if you start the day with a positive frame of mind, your feeling of well-being can slip away as the day wears on. This is when many people allow their positive attitudes to slip away also; however, this is exactly the right time to think differently. You are responsible for being in control of the way you act and live your life.

If you feel depression or anger coming on because of how a project has gone or because of something someone said, don't do what you normally do (like take your frustrations out on a sympathetic person, spouse, or coworker). Instead, take a few moments to breathe. Take a walk outside or to another part of the building. Sip a glass of water to cool down. Don't drink coffee; you don't need to feel more jittery. Have some uplifting words handy to read. In other words, physically take action to lift your mood.

When you are feeling down, that's *exactly the time you can make a difference!* You are responsible for you. Nobody else can do it for you. You deserve to be happy. You deserve to have a positive frame of mind. You deserve to be the best that you can be! Here are some exercises to help you maintain the right attitude.

AFFIRMATIONS FOR MAINTAINING THE RIGHT ATTITUDE

1. I want to help.
2. I'm happy to make a difference.
3. I maintain a good, positive frame of mind.
4. I am always prepared.
5. I am sincere.
6. My energy is uplifting.
7. I take time to breathe and control my response.

Thoughts to Avoid

You know them already—so we won't even highlight them!

CHECK-IN

We learn by example. Make a list of people who manage to keep a positive attitude, even when they are tired. Ask yourself these questions:

1. What makes them seem so positive?
2. Are they more outgoing?
3. Do they smile more?
4. Are they giving?
5. Do they go with the flow?
6. Do they make an effort to go forward with a better attitude?
7. When they are angry, do they get rid of it quickly?
8. If someone insults them, do they take it personally or shrug it off?

ACTION

Which skills do *you* need? How can you learn these skills? If you need to smile more, do it. If you need to take things less personally, do it. Walk past a group of people and say, "Are we all happy?" But here's the test: You have to say it with sincerity—as if you really want them to be; as if you are sharing your happiness with them.

ACTION

Super Service is about having an amazing life, not just at work, but with your family and friends. Be the person who gives good, positive energy. Don't be the one who takes energy, who always has a problem, and who constantly finds fault. You were born to be amazing. Let your amazing personality shine forth.

Write down in the space below, what you will do today and for the rest of your life to manifest your amazing personality.

_____

_____

_____

Chapter 4

CUSTOMER SERVICE KEY 2

Understand the Customer's Needs

Imagining what it is like to be your customer
is a powerful customer service technique.

Here is how two of our clients, who participated in our *Super Service* workshop, answered three questions:

Thomas—Computer Associates, Event Strategy

1. **As a customer, what do you want?**
   "Polite, helpful service."
2. **As a customer, what do you feel stops you from getting what you want?**
   "My attitude in expecting good polite, helpful service."
3. **In your experience, what do customer service people do best?**
   "Respond to my friendly attitude/comments with friendly, polite, helpful service."

Carmen—McDonald's Corporation, Service Center

1. **As a customer, what do you want?**
   "A service provider that makes me feel appreciated and helped."
2. **As a customer, what do you feel stops you from getting what you want?**
   "Impatience."
3. **In your experience, what do customer service people do best?**
   "Provide a service to assist with information at the customer's request."

Up-Selling

My niece's 17-year-old son was staying with us for a couple of weeks. He was here from the United Kingdom on a work experience and I asked him, "So what do you think of service in America?"

"It's good, but its phony isn't it?" he said. I asked him what he meant exactly and he told me about his experience of going into a fast-food restaurant and ordering a hamburger. "The girl was saying all the right things, but she didn't care about me. She was just telling me what she had been told to say." So I asked him what it was like in England and he said, "Oh, it's really bad over there. You don't get any service at all." Of course, it's always easier to be critical of the system that you know. I know from traveling worldwide that service is pretty much the same in every part of the world. It's all about attitude—some people have a great attitude and others do not.

I asked him, "Do you prefer to get no service or service from people pretending to give you service, even if they don't mean it?"

"I like it better if they pretend," and then he added, "I just hate it when they list off all these products I don't want. She asked me if I wanted a drink with it, fries, or a dessert—I just wanted to order my burger!"

"It's up-selling," I said. "Did you buy anything she suggested?"

"No," he said. "And if I went there again and they kept asking me if I wanted this other stuff, I'd get really mad."

Some places train their service providers to up-sell regardless of the signals that the customer is giving off. It would be better to say to their staff, "We want you to offer these additional products, but please use your common sense; if it's obvious that customers are getting frustrated, then, just give them what they asked for."

We joke about it and even write songs about it, like Jon Bon Jovi singing "Have a Nice Day" in an angry kind of way. But really, it is better to at least pretend to be of service than to not bother. It is better to create a buying environment, which tends to help customers get more out of the products and services they bought from you in the first place.

▼

KEY POINT

Use your common sense with creating a buying environment. Give customers what they want. If you are obviously annoying and frustrating customers when you keep asking if they want additional products, then don't offer them.

I have a friend who coaches restaurant owners in Australia, and he told me, "one restaurant owner has her staff say: "Leave some room for dessert; we have some delicious desserts on the menu tonight." Just saying those few words has a big effect on customers; they often do get dessert and the restaurant's bottom line has increased. The servers are planting a seed, "oh yes, I'd love some dessert." That's how creating a buying environment works; a suggestion of something delicious, rather than an annoying list of other foods on the menu.

Anger and the Immune System

Giving *Super Service* makes everyone feel good—the customer; the service provider, the line-manager and the owner. When people don't give *Super Service*, everyone feels bad, but the one who is most affected is the service provider and here's why: He or she is the one who has to deal with angry thoughts, being upset, and feeling bad. The customer can walk away thinking, "wow that was a really bad experience." The customer has the choice whether to complain, walk away, or find another vendor. The service provider has to stay and serve the next customer. If the service provider feels angry, he or she has to stay and deal with the effect.

Here is a statistic about anger and its effect on our bodies which blew my mind, maybe yours too!

> *"Five minutes of strong negative emotions, such as anger, will knock out the immune system for six hours. Therefore, 20 minutes of strong negative emotions will suppress the immune system for one entire day."*

The results are based on research done by the International College of Integrative Medicine located in Tampa, Florida. They measured the level of salivary Immunoglobulin A and found: "After only five minutes of being angry, it takes six hours for salivary Immunoglobulin A (IgA, an important protective chemical produced by your immune system) to return to baseline."

The immune system is one of the most complex systems of the human body. It is composed of lymphatic vessels and organs, white blood cells, and specialized cells. Its prime function is to protect the body against infection and the development of cancer.

We have this amazing immune system which is designed to protect us from life-threatening invaders, but the problem is that it reacts like an over-diligent parent; it errs on the side of caution and sometimes sees things as threats or enemies when they're really not. In other words, our immune system is designed to overreact! The core of the immune system is the fight or flight response. We see a threat and we either fight or run. This response was formed in the last major evolutionary development of humans, somewhere between 35,000 and 120,000 years ago; it was designed for life in small clan clusters where everything outside the clan was viewed as a threat to survival. It didn't make sense in those days to take a chance on the peaceful intent of a stranger. The survival response of the animal brain is to attack first and play it safe.

▼

KEY POINT

Five minutes of strong negative emotions, such as anger, will knock out the immune system for six hours. Therefore, 20 minutes of strong negative emotions will suppress the immune system for one entire day.

Today, most people are not threatened unless they are at war. We enjoy having the emotional closeness and the emotional safety of being with family, friends, coworkers, and customers. The problem is that the biological design of our emotional immune system is in favor of our physical protection. We are designed to assume danger so we fight, get angry, become critical, and sarcastic; or we flee by emotionally withdrawing, avoiding, or turning away.

We've talked about it in Chapter 1, animal brain versus human brain; the only way a customer service provider can really create a win-win situation is to operate from his or her human brain so that the immune system stays healthy. It is just not worth it to get angry. This is not even about customer service; this is about you and your health. So to be healthy, keep your sense of humor, and always ask yourself; "Is this worth shutting down my immune system and creating a possibility of disease?"

Other people's shoes rarely fit. If we want to understand people better, we have to make allowances. Have you ever been told to "put yourself in their position" or "stand in their shoes"? What does this really mean?

Understanding someone else's experience is impossible unless it has happened to us, and even then the experience will be different. What we can do, though, is imagine. "Imagining what it is like to be your customer" is a powerful customer service technique. It is a first step toward understanding the customer's needs.

Prepare for a Customer Interaction

Another more concrete trick for understanding customer needs is to keep a file for each of your external customers. Use the files (or your company's existing files for customers) to hold information that will help you remember them and understand their past problems and concerns. This will help you understand your customer's needs better during your next conversation. Before a meeting, review the file and get to know the customer's product or service history. Understand past problems, recommendations, and solutions.

In our experience, there is nothing worse than a service provider who has not done his or her homework before talking to a customer. A woman friend told us about a recent experience when her doctor asked, "Everything okay with your period?" "I had a hysterectomy two years ago!" she replied. This does not make for a good doctor–patient relationship. We can be effective only when we have done our customer homework. In the example of the doctor and patient, the information must have been in the patient's file. Why didn't the doctor take the time to read it? Being "too busy" is not a good answer. How can service providers ask the right questions when they have the wrong (or no) information?

Is it different for people who deal with a large number of unknown customers each day and who do not form long-term personal relationships? Yes and no. Obviously, we cannot know personal details of customers we may speak to only once every two months. What we should know, however, is:

1. Typical problems and how to resolve them.
2. The options available to our customers.
3. Past case histories.

Preparation means knowing in advance what might come up. It doesn't take long to do, but in terms of *Super Service* it is time very well spent.

How to Listen with an Open Mind

An "open mind" is one that is open to new experiences and new ideas, like an empty vessel ready to be filled. (Remember that, by being "no thing," you can be "every thing" for your customer.) Listen to your customer's problem with an open mind, and, as you listen, fill your mind with the problem. Only when you have the complete problem should you begin to think of a solution.

Unfortunately, the mind is so resistant to remaining empty and being filled with another person's problem that it fills itself up with solutions. Then, desperately wanting to pour itself out, the mind overwhelms listeners with a "flash flood" of solutions.

So how do you retain an open mind? How do you remain open to listening to your customers, to really hear what they are saying before you interrupt and drown them out? Here is a visualization technique to follow when talking with a customer:

When you are steering the boat, you have the power to take it wherever you want to go. The customers can row and row and use up as much energy as they want, but they cannot get to their destination without you steering there. But the object of steering is to land safely—by solving the customer's problem. It is a huge responsibility and you need to have some skills—in your case, listening and question-asking skills.

VISUALIZATION TECHNIQUE—TALKING WITH CUSTOMERS

1. Think of the conversation as a gentle flowing river.
2. You and your customer are in one boat; you are steering.
3. Your job is to help the boat stay free from obstructions.
4. You steer with gentle direction.
5. Your goal is to land safely and peacefully at the other end.
6. You never need to use force or too much energy.
7. If the river goes too fast, you are still able to steer the boat safely and keep it under control until you get to calmer water.
8. You have the capability and the energy.
9. You have the strength.
10. You have the will.

Here is a technique you can practice. It is easier with an internal customer or, better still, a close friend or significant other. This is what you do:

- Look into the other person's eyes when he or she is talking to you.
- Do not look away.
- Focus all your attention on the speaker.
- Do not allow your mind to wander.
- When it wanders, bring it back to focus on the other person.
- Listen not just to the words, but to the body language.
- Is the speaker closed (look at legs and arms) toward you or open?

- Is he fidgeting, scratching his head, or peaceful?
- Is she saying peaceful words but fidgeting?
- Do his words mirror his body language?
- Is she saying how she really feels?
- How can you help the customer express his feelings?
- How can you stop yourself from taking her comments personally?

The last question in this exercise, about *not taking things personally,* is perhaps the hardest component of listening. As soon as we feel threatened or criticized, a huge voice in our head screams at us, "Attack, attack, attack!" This is quickly followed by another huge voice, "Defend, defend, defend!"

If we are not self-aware, we listen to this voice and quickly go from "listening" to "defending" or even "attacking." We will even interrupt the speaker, "Just a minute! That never happened like that. I never said that. It wasn't me." By the time we get defensive, it has become almost impossible for us to offer *Super Service.* The alternative is to get outside our own feelings and focus on the customer's needs.

Understand What a Need Is

To understand the customer's needs, we have to completely rid our mind of what *we think* he or she wants and replace it with what he or she *really* wants.

For example, Cindy knows we want to have our dry cleaning the next day, even though we often don't pick it up until the following week. Is this a headache for her? Sometimes it must be, especially if the dry cleaner is very busy.

Cindy has worked out that we are very good customers. We are loyal, we are regular, we smile, and we always pay cash so she doesn't have to bother with credit cards or checks. It is worth her time to give us what we want, which is the comfort of knowing our clothes are clean and available should something unexpected happen, like being called out of town.

In order to understand your customer's needs, you must look beyond the strict definition of your company's product or service. Here is what you should do:

Listen for what the customer really needs/wants/desires.

If you are not listening closely, you may provide a basic need, but miss the chance to satisfy a customer's desire! Because the word "desire" is so alien in a book about customer care, we will continue to use the accepted word "need." However, remember that needs represent wants and desires.

Verify and Clarify Needs

One way to check whether you have answered your customer's needs is to clarify the facts. This means restating details, such as numbers, spellings of names and addresses, quantities, timelines, dates, delivery needs, etc.

- *"I understand:* There were 15 parts delivered and you needed 25. *Is that correct?"*
- *"Let me see if I understand.* You paid the bill on March 1st, and your last statement didn't reflect this?"
- *"So, what you're saying,* John, is that when the thermostat is on high, it blows out cold air. *Have I got it right?"*

When you clarify the facts in this way, you are on the way to making sure that all of their needs/wants/desires are met. For example, Cindy, the dry cleaner, could say to us, "Five days is too long to wait for the dry cleaning. You want it the next day, correct?" It's a feel-good thing. The customer can breathe a sigh of relief: Aaahh, this person knows what I *really* want.

Barriers to Problem Solving

Some of the barriers to problem solving arise from the *customer's attitude*. For example, the customer:

- Does not want to work with you.
- Wants to work against you.
- Does not trust you.
- Does not respect your ability to help.

The only way to overcome these types of attitudes is to keep your mind focused on the goal: *to help solve the customer's problem.* If you can do this, you will remain unaffected by the customer's attitude. This focus will help you be objective and not take things personally. Remember, to customers you represent your company. You could be a saint, but customers will still regard you with distrust if that is what they have in *their* mind.

Another barrier to solving problems is *not taking responsibility*. Customers must know that you have taken responsibility for helping them, that you want to correctly diagnose their problem, and that you want to provide the right solution.

In trying to explain the problem, the customer may have difficulty organizing his or her thoughts. You may hear phrases such as:

"It's very confusing . . ."
"I just can't figure it out . . ."
"I'm not sure how to . . ."
"It doesn't seem to . . ."

Be patient. Remember, you know all about your product; your customer may not. Here are some tips:

1. Speak slowly.
2. Use short sentences.
3. Be tactful.
4. Ask, "Do you have any questions?" or "Am I being clear?"

Most barriers to problems begin and end with people. We must realize that nothing remains the same, that life is about change, and that change brings its own set of problems. Only then can we learn to have a realistic attitude. Then each problem becomes a wonderful opportunity to act in the way we want to be.

Each problem is an opportunity to react as we would expect a peaceful person to react. If we want to become peaceful, it's no good being peaceful all alone on the top of a mountain. The only way to become peaceful is to do so in the middle of a difficult problem.

How we choose to handle problems is up to us, and the beautiful and liberating thing is that we *can* change. Every moment we have the opportunity to redo our lives. Every moment we can have another go at becoming the person we feel we are inside. The only thing we really need to do is wake up to who we really are!

Honesty as a Tool

If you truly want to help others, you can begin by doing these three things:

1. Think kind thoughts.
2. Speak gently.
3. Use wisdom.

Everything you are inside is reflected in how you treat people. It is almost impossible to think gentle thoughts and act with anger. Alternatively, it is very difficult to think angry thoughts and act with peace. Often our words become a reflection of our ego; they build up the walls around our concept of "me," "mine," and "I am a very important person, don't mess with me!"

Begin today to speak the truth. If your product or service has created a problem for your customer, you must acknowledge it. If a customer is distraught about the problem, you must help him or her through it.

Customers have much more faith in a company that is "big" enough to say, "Yes, we made a mistake, and we have enough strength and power behind us to *make good.*"

ACTION

It would be a very boring life if we thought of customers as nonbeings, as if they were numbers to "chalk up." We need to personalize our interactions with customers, so that our lives become more interesting and meaningful.

Today and for the rest of your life, do these two things:

1. Become open to listening.
2. Listen for what your customers are feeling, not just for their words.

When you truly listen to others, you will hear "between the lines." You will sense where the words are coming from, rather than just hearing the words. You will feel what others are feeling, and you will be able to respond as a human being responds to a call for help from a child—unselfishly, ready to serve, and wanting to be your best.

ACTION

You know that being angry closes down your immune system, which can create disease in your mind and body. In other words, it is not good for you.

Write down one main action that you will take in order to stop yourself from being angry.

taking a deep breath, changing position, or taking a sip of water

Chapter 5

CUSTOMER SERVICE KEY 3

Communicate Clearly

We sometimes overwhelm our customer with too much
information. Always think KISS! **Keep It Simple and Sincere!**

Here is how two of our clients, who participated in our *Super Service* workshop, answered the following three questions:

Carol—GE Healthcare Financial Services, Customer Transaction Coordinator

1. **As a customer, what do you want?**

   "I want to be treated as if I'm the most important person in the world."

2. **As a customer, what do you feel stops you from getting what you want?**

   "I sometimes feel as if no one is listening to my request and I have to keep repeating myself."

3. **In your experience, what do customer service people do best?**

   "Listen and treat the customer as if they are the only person in the world."

Arron—Computer Associates, Support Engineer

1. **As a customer, what do you want?**

   "As a customer, all I ever ask is for friendly, reliable service. I don't always need to get the answer right away, or my order does not need to be correct every time. I just want the person providing a service to me to genuinely care about the service she is providing me. If the service provider cares about the customer, the customer will usually be satisfied."

2. **As a customer, what do you feel stops you from getting what you want?**

   "Bad service! If the service is careless, or inattentive, then there is no way I am getting what I want."

3. **In your experience, what do customer service people do best?**

   "Well, if you mean GOOD customer service people, then what they do best is to take ownership of your problem or question and see it through to resolution or completion. This usually goes hand in hand with being interested and attentive to the customer's needs. When I get on the phone with say, customer support for my computer, when the representative tells me something like, 'Okay I am going to get this problem taken care of for you,' I immediately know I am in good hands."

Getting to "Yes"

Most people know that John Lennon married Yoko Ono, but do you know how he fell in love with her? It was 1966 and he was in a London art gallery looking at one of her pieces of art. She had arranged it so that viewers had to climb to the top of a shaky ladder, in a dimly lit room, and look through a spyglass to a small part of the ceiling. This created the idea of a dark, dangerous, and unstable world where the power of a single word would create a healing effect.

If you don't know the story, you might think the word was "love," but it was something much more interesting, and it made Lennon begin to emotionally fall for the woman who had arranged for it to be seen in that way.

The word was "yes."

It is a simple word, and there has been a lot of research about it. We are going to provide you with the information that will help you communicate in such a way, so that people say "yes" to your thoughts and ideas. Here they are.

How Can I Help?

Like President John F. Kennedy once famously said, "Ask not what your country can do for you. Ask what you can do for your country." If you want to influence customers, coworkers, your boss, family, and friends, ask yourself: "How can I help?" or, "What favor can I give?"

Helping others is about providing useful information, and a friendly, listening ear. Specifically, helping people creates:

1. A social obligation for them to help or support you at a future date.
2. A cooperative environment which will serve you when you need assistance.
3. The need to reciprocate when important projects need to be completed.
4. A healthy network of indebted colleagues who are more responsive to your requests.

Make Your Opening Words Count

From a *Super Service* perspective, when you are friendly, polite, and responsive at the beginning of an interaction, you are more likely to have a good interaction. So for example, use words like: "Thank you for calling," or, "How may I help you?" "We appreciate your business . . ."

Pay attention to your own experience of customer service. Pay attention to how other CSRs answer the telephone. What works for you? What does not work for you?

What tips can you pick up from your experience with customer service? *Super Service* is about connecting with other people in a way that is helpful and productive. It's not about using "canned" phrases that roll off the tip of your tongue without even thinking about what you are saying. That gets very boring for yourself and your customer—and the last thing we want in *Super Service* is to be bored, or indifferent.

Getting Bigger Tips

You've most likely been to restaurants and seen the mints placed in a basket near the door. But did you know studies show that "gift" candy has a huge impact on the customers tip? The cost of these little candies may only be a few pennies, but how and when the server gives them has a huge impact. Here are the results:

1. A single piece of candy is given with the bill. (Tip increases by 3.3 percent.)
2. Two pieces of candy are given to each diner at the table. (Tip increases by 14.1 percent.)
3. Server gives one piece of candy per diner, turns away as if leaving, then turns back, reaches into pocket and gives a second piece, as if to say "Here's an extra piece of candy. You're such great customers." (Tip increases by 23 perent.)

Obviously, we're not advocating using these tricks in a cunning or manipulative way; that would only backfire. However, you can use them in an ethical way to show your appreciation to your patron.

More on Tips

Here is some research gathered from food servers. When a waiter repeats the customer's order back to him or her **exactly** as the customer said it, it can increase the size of the tip by 70 percent, as opposed to if the waiter nods, paraphrases, says "okay" or "coming up."

No String Incentives

Have you been to a hotel that has towel reuse programs? They have cards to remind patrons about the importance of protecting the environment by reusing towels and saving energy. Some hotels even offer incentives: "The hotel will donate a percentage of energy savings to a nonprofit environmental protection organization."

But studies show that if the hotel has ALREADY donated on behalf of their guests, and asks the guests to reciprocate this gesture by reusing their towels during their stay, 45 percent of guests are more likely to reuse their towels. How is this so?

When you ask for cooperation from coworkers, clients, students, or acquaintances, it's better to offer help in a way that has *no* strings attached. In other words, change the sequence. *Give then Ask*, instead of *Ask then Give*: "I've called the first list of clients we talked about. Could you help me with the second list?"

Giving and Getting Favors

When you do someone a favor, the person receiving it values it greatly at the time, but as time goes by he or she is likely to forget it. But for you, the person giving the favor, it has exactly the opposite effect. You don't value it highly at the time, but as time passes by, you put more value on the favor you did.

You can imagine how this can affect relationships:

You: "Remember when I helped you with your proposal?"
Them: "No, I don't remember."
You: "You don't remember—I spent all day working on it!!"

The way not to fall into this problem is as follows:

1. Tell the person you are doing the favor for, "Of course, I'll help with the proposal. I'm sure if the situation were reversed, you'd do the same for me."
2. Remind the person of the value of the favor, "Did it help get the contract, me working on the proposal with you? Good! I need a favor too . . ."

Using the Right Label

In one of the *Star Wars* movies, Luke Skywalker turned to Darth Vader and said, "I know there's good still in you. There's good in you, I can sense it." Luke was planting the seeds of persuasion. This is known as the "labeling technique" and it has been proven to work.

For example, research showed that a group of children who were told, "You're just the kind of students who care about having good handwriting," spent more free time practicing their handwriting—even when there was no one around to watch.

Airlines that say, "We know you have many airlines to choose from, so we thank you for choosing ours," are reminding customers that they chose the airline for a good reason—which makes customers continue to justify their own confidence in the airline.

Use the labeling technique in delivering *Super Service*—it works:

"Thank you for bringing this to my attention, I appreciate your concern."
"Thank you for choosing us."
" I appreciate your continued business."

Motivating People to Keep Reservations

When it comes to keeping reservations, customers sometimes have a hard time remembering the appointment. That's why many salons employ staff just to call up the day before to remind clients of the reservation. But did you know that customers, who commit themselves by saying "yes" to the question, feel the need to be consistent with their commitment? Here is a study on how receptionists called clients to confirm their appointment:

1. "Please call if you have to cancel." (30 percent no-show rate)
2. "Will you please call if you have to cancel?" (10 percent no-show rate)

Writing Down Your Commitment

Amway is one of America's most profitable direct-selling companies. Here's how they encourage their sales personnel.

> One final tip before you get started: Set a goal and write it down. Whatever the goal, the important thing is that you set it, so you've got something for which to aim—and that you write it down. There is something magical about writing things down. So set a goal and write it down. When you reach that goal, set another and write it down. You'll be off and running.

It's all about the words you use. Researchers set up a study with a group of students which shows the importance of writing things down. Both groups were told if they want to volunteer they should:

Group 1: "Fill out a form stating that you are willing to participate."(49 percent turned up.)

Group 2: "Leave the form blank stating that you are not willing to participate."(17 percent turned up.)

Retailers find that customers are more likely to keep agreements (financial or otherwise) if they fill out the application form themselves. Health care providers report that more patients keep their appointments when the patients fill out the card themselves, rather than the receptionist or administrator.

▼

KEY POINT

If you want to influence others effectively, have them write it down. Psychologically, it's a significant action that can make all the difference in whether people turn up or not.

Every Bit Will Help

Researchers found that when asking people to give donations, a simple change in the wording made all the difference:

1. "Would you be willing to help by giving a donation?"(28.6 percent gave a donation.)
2. "Would you be willing to help by giving a donation? Even a penny will help." (50 percent gave a donation.)

Even though the second group were more likely to give donations, when they were told, "every penny will help," the size of donations was the same with both groups. Here's how this can help with delivering *Super Service*:

1. "Just an hour of your time will really help."
2. "It will be very helpful, if we can go over this."
3. "Yes, a little more clarity will help."
4. "Thank you, a brief telephone call will definately help."

KEY POINT

Every journey begins with one small step. If you can get people to take one little step with you, they may end up going the whole journey.

Mirroring

An experiment was made with Master in Business Administration (MBA) students; two groups were involved in making a deal and each were given a different set of instructions as follows:

Group 1: Subtly mirror the person—lean forward or back to match the other person. (They reached a deal 67 percent of the time.)

Group 2: Do not mirror the person. (They reached a deal 12.5 percent of the time.)

Mirroring a person leads to increased trust and a willingness to disclose details that may otherwise remain hidden.

Our work with clients often requires us to review recorded telephone conversations between customers and customer service reps (CSRs). This one really gives strength to the power of mirroring—or in this particular case *not* mirroring.

Customer:	"Your company promised to resolve this situation, and nothing's happened. I'm really angry."
CSR:	"I'm sorry you're annoyed."
Customer:	"I'm not annoyed, I'm angry."
CSR:	"Yes, I understand you're upset."
Customer:	"Upset! Don't tell me what I am. I am not upset. I am angry! Get me the manager!"

Conversations like this can easily spiral out of control, because the CSR did not acknowledge that the customer was angry. To use the mirroring technique in a situation like this simply say,

"I'm sorry that you are angry. My name is Joy. What can we do together to resolve the situation?"

KEY POINT

Repeating the customer's words can help resolve a situation, build rapport and a stronger relationship.

The Power of an Authentic Smile

Chinese proverb: "Don't open a shop unless you like to smile."

A friendly local sandwich place Jeff and I always go into had been recently taken over; so we went in to see what it was like. The young man at the counter looked up and said, "Hi, just choose off the menu and we'll bring it to the table." No smile. Above him was a framed newspaper clipping, showing his picture—he was standing behind the counter, but he wasn't smiling even in the picture! And he didn't seem happy to see us. When we finished eating, I looked at Jeff and said, "Would you come back?" He said no, and I said, "Me neither."

What a shame! The food was good, but who wants to eat in a place where the people aren't happy to see you?

I know, sometimes we feel so bad in our lives that it is even difficult to fake a smile. In these situations, try the Benjamin Franklin approach, "Search others for their virtues." In other words, if you can't find anything to smile about and you are being approached by a customer or client, look for something good about them—"I like your coat!" It's no good being inauthentic; people smell it a mile away. But you can always find something to like about another person! A item of clothing, a piece of jewelry, there's always something to like about people.

Keep It Simple and Sincere

We have the power to make our customers feel good or bad just by the way we communicate. Here are a few rules about giving information:

1. **Be clear.** Use simple words without any jargon.
2. **Stick to the point.** Keep focused on the problem and the solution.
3. **Be honest.** It's dangerous to overpromise and underperform.

There are also a few phrases to avoid when giving information:

1. **"I'll be honest with you."** Saying this sounds like you haven't been honest until now.
2. **"I can't."** This is like putting a brick wall up between you and your customer. State what you can do, rather than what you can't!
3. **"I'll let you know."** When will you get back? Give a date and a time. Make it happen!

Because information is power, we sometimes overwhelm our customer with too much information. In an attempt to impress, we may use too many technical terms or jargon. **K**eep **I**t **S**imple and **S**incere, or **KISS**. Winston Churchill, one of the great communicators of our time, always wrote his speeches for the comprehension level of a 12-year-old. Another master communicator was Benjamin Franklin. He felt voters' rights should not be predicated on ownership of property. His supporters drafted a "white paper" that was overly done and pompous. He rewrote it in an easier way: "I own a mule, I can vote. My mule dies, I cannot vote! Therefore the vote represents not me, but my mule!"

Be like Benjamin Franklin and get rid of redundant language. Here are examples:

Redundant	Use Instead
Assemble together	Assemble
General consensus of opinion	Consensus
Red in color	Red
Basic fundamentals	Fundamentals
Important essentials	Essentials
Due to the fact that	Because
In the event that	If
I am in receipt of	I received

Here are more examples of unnecessary words:

Instead of	Use
We made a recommendation	We recommended
We entered into discussion	We discussed
We made an inspection	We inspected
We performed a study	We studied

There are many ways to speak to be understood. The simplest way is to use few words, short words, and short sentences.

Resist using technical terms and jargon. You probably know all about your product or service and are familiar with the industry jargon. Your company may even have its own language. Because you are so familiar with all of these terms, you expect your customers to be. But imagine if doctors had the same expectation. They have every right to; after all, they are dealing with *our bodies*! This equipment carries us around every day; it's our vehicle! We may not know how a DVD player works, but our own bodies? Not so! If the doctor talked to us in medical jargon, we might think we had only a couple of months to live: "So my eye infection is caused by all these microorganisms feeding on the *what*?"

Always think KISS: **K**eep **I**t **S**imple and **S**incere! Here's a technique to help you. On the checklist below, write down your explanation of how your product or service operates.

PRODUCT OR SERVICE PROFILE

Write your explanation of how your product or service operates.

My product/service is called: _____

_____

It works by: _____

_____

Its benefits are: _____

_____

It solves problems by: _____

_____

Other information to add is: _____

_____

Now go back and edit your Product or Service Profile using the following suggestions:

1. **Choose the most familiar words.** If you shouted, "Quick, there's a conflagration!" many people would not know what to do. Why not shout "Fire"?
2. **Eliminate jargon.** Take out any word that looks strange.
3. **Build a foundation of key words.** In school you had to be creative: You were taught to say the same thing a different way each time. In the real world it is very different: You need to be direct (short and simple is always best).
4. **Trim your sentences.** A long sentence is like nonstop talk. Chop the sentences up to average 15 to 18 words per sentence.

Next time you have to explain your product or service to a customer, use your edited version. It will help you, and it will help them understand what you are talking about. No one likes to ask questions because they don't know the jargon—so don't use it.

How to Give Unwelcome Information

We all make mistakes, and sometimes we have to give information that the customer does not want to hear. You must do two things:

1. Accept responsibility.
2. Be direct.

As human beings, we "smell" fear, and it makes us fearful. We see bad news coming and get agitated, so the best way is to get right to the point.

For example, you gave the customer a wrong delivery charge and you cannot adjust it. Using the direct approach, you say, "I'm sorry, I made an error when I quoted the delivery charge. I quoted you $60, and the correct price is $75. I apologize for the mistake and hope it won't cause a problem." People make mistakes, we all know that, and if you own up to the mistake, people are much more likely to forgive you.

Try to explain the situation in positive rather than negative terms. Which of the following sentences sounds like the person likes the raincoat?

"This raincoat keeps the water out, *but* it's short."

"This raincoat keeps the water out, *and* it's short."

The bottom one is much more positive! When we use the word "but," we are eliminating anything good we have said—but is like saying 'no.' "This raincoat keeps the water out, *but* . . ." means that we don't like the raincoat, even if it does keep the water out. "This raincoat keeps the water out, *and* . . ." means that not only does it keep the water out, but it also has another positive element! Notice when people use the word "but" and listen to what they are really saying. Notice what you are *really* saying when *you* use the word "but."

Good News/Bad News Approach

The good news/bad news approach is an old cliché, and we don't want to say to our customers, "Do you want the good news first, or the bad news?" However, good news/ bad news can help in some cases. For example, "To help your situation I've brought the installation forward by two days. However, I apologize for a mistake I made with the delivery charge. The correct price is $75 instead of $60. I'm sorry for the error and any inconvenience."

When we make an error, it is important to accept responsibility for it. If we can sweeten the bad news for the customer, so much the better. That's all!

Encourage the Customer to Participate in Finding the Right Solution

When you involve the customer in finding the right solution, the customer is more likely to want the solution to work. Give your customers verbal or nonverbal clues to encourage their participation:

"You mentioned an alternative solution earlier. What did you have in mind?"
"That's interesting. Can you tell me more about that?"

Acknowledge the Customer's Feelings

We can go to a thousand seminars and read a million books about customer care. But until we acknowledge that customers are people and that people have feelings, we may as well throw our money to the wind.

Customers want to know that you are listening to their problem, and that you understand the problem is causing grief. You are not saying, "I understand how you feel," because you may not understand how they feel—they could be going through all kinds of problems that you have never experienced—but you can empathize, because we all know what it is like to have problems that are difficult to fix.

A few days ago I had a problem with a telephone company; I kept calling and repeating the problem to different people, but I wasn't getting any joy—I was really fed up because it was affecting my business. Then this one CSR said, "If that happened to me, I would feel the same way, my name is Paul, and my job is to find a solution." And he did, it was fantastic—finally someone who appreciated how frustrated I felt.

Know When to Call in the Manager

At times you have to call in the manager. A manager can bring a new perspective to the situation. A manager can also give the customer more confidence that the problem will be solved.

It is appropriate to call the manager if:

The customer is very angry.
If you have tried every solution possible.
If the customer is still not satisfied.

If retail employees had to pick one common phrase they would prefer not to hear from a customer, it would be, "I'd like to speak to a manager." While retail salespeople may complain about customers who demand to see the boss, managers should go the extra mile to embrace these argumentative or difficult shoppers. It's always better to pacify angry customers than watch them storm off, never to return.

As a rule of thumb, it's only a customer who cares about a business who will actually complain, so when someone asks to see the manager that means they're upset about the treatment or service they're getting, So the most important thing for the employee to say is, "No problem," and go get the manager.

Watch your attitude in these situations—don't take anything personally. In this case, the old adage, "It's not what you say, it's how you say it" applies. So be cordial, go get the manager, and then excuse yourself from the situation.

CHECK-IN

Write down the top three problems your customers encounter:

1. _____

2. _____

3. _____

Now write down the solutions and pin them up so you know how to answer them the next time the problem occurs:

1. _____

2. _____

3. _____

Chapter 6

Reach Agreement

Incorporate the customer's ideas into your solution.

Here is how one of our clients, who participated in our *Super Service* workshop, answered the following three questions:

Roger—GE Healthcare Financial Services, Modality Product Leader

1. **As a customer, what do you want?**

   "I want to feel that I am being helped, not being a source of income. For example, recently I had an issue with a leaky toilet at one of the rental properties that I own. The plumbing company, who had just installed that toilet a few months ago, insisted the failure was not their fault and I would have to pay the bill. Even though their bill was small compared to the $5,000 damage the leaky toilet caused, they stuck to their guns on not helping us by minimizing our bill . . . even though we have a major bathroom remodel planned for our own home bathroom. Little did they know that they will be losing the $6,000 plumbing project . . . and mind you we have already spent thousands and thousands of dollars with this firm on our properties. It just seems that many businesses are more in the mode of helping themselves instead of their customers."

2. **As a customer, what do you feel stops you from getting what you want?**

   "As a customer, I hate to say it, but people seem entirely focused on their own little worlds . . . I was refused access to my vision prescription over the phone last week . . . the representative told me that HIPPA prevented her from providing that information to me . . . now while I know what 'HIPPA' is, (Health Insurance Portability and Accountability Act) I don't think most people would, but she automatically assumed her little world of lingo was the same as her customers."

3. **In your experience, what do customer service people do best?**

   "Good customer service people help us with the unexpected . . . like an insurance agent several years ago who out of the blue told us she was looking at our insurance to see where we could save money with the same or better coverage . . . and saved us hundreds of dollars and with better coverage! So, to sum it up . . . look at the big picture with your customers, try to relate to them, and go out of your way to provide the unexpected 'win' for them."

Here is how a subscriber to our newsletter at www.winnersattitude.com answered the first question; he didn't give his company name or title, we just know him as "Randi B."

Randi B.
1. **As a customer, what do you want?**
    "To be made to feel special, as if I mattered, and that I was the most important person that they had to take care of. Oh, and thank me for my business, because I could take it elsewhere, if the service I receive from you isn't good enough . . . whether you think you can, or you think you can't, you're right."

Eight Tools to Reach Agreement

As the great Albert Einstein said, "There are two ways to live your life. One is as though nothing is a miracle. The other is as though everything is a miracle." I wholeheartedly agree, but sometimes, the animal brain takes over and life seems to be one great big struggle. And when you are struggling to get what you want, everything seems to be against you. People take advantage of you. You feel like you have to fight aggressively for what you want, bend over backwards, or form an alliance with people you don't like. Sometimes, you need help from people, but don't have any direct authority over them. Whatever the scenario, here are eight simple but effective tools for getting back into your human brain.

1. **Write down your goal.** What do you want? What do you think the other person, your customer, wants? Do this before a meeting, a telephone call, or even at the beginning of each day. Know what you want and what you are going to do to get it.
    > "Today I want to provide polite, fast service, resolve customer problems, and feel great at the end of the day."
    > "Today I want to have a great day, find solutions, be amazing for my customers, and go home feeling good about myself."
2. **Trade.** What do you and your customer have that you can trade? What do you each have that the other wants? As far as *Super Service* goes, you are trading your energy, patience, and ability to find solutions. Your customer is trading their money, time, and effort—without the customer you would not have a job, and if you didn't have a job, you would have no money. It's a good place to start. Think good positive thoughts and be willing to do your job with a smile on your face. As a customer, I know, and you know it takes a lot of effort and energy to complain, so appreciate the effort they are taking to resolve their problem—it is their effort that has given you a job in customer service.

3. **Agreement.** Most of your *Super Service* transactions need to end in agreement. With competition the way it is today, customers can always find another product, service, or person to provide them with the service they need. If you don't reach agreement with this customer, it's going to create a lot of trouble for your co-workers down the line. I've made calls as a customer and been handed to several different people to explain the problem over and over again—when a customer comes to you, and IF you can't handle the problem, make sure you pass them along to the right person who can—if possible give the next person a "heads up." If you can't, apologize for the need to pass them along, and tell them the information they will need to provide—maybe they don't need to tell the whole story—just a certain part of it.

4. **Relationships.** What is the history of the relationship with this customer? How does this history impact the situation? Are there any hidden issues that may influence the situation? How will you handle these? It's not just about your personal relationship with the customer, but it's also about their relationship with your company. Whether someone has been a customer for a short time, or for a long time, in both cases, this customer expects the very best *Super Service* from you.

5. **Expected outcomes.** What outcome does your customer expect from this situation? What has the outcome been in the past, and what precedents have been set? Of course, you don't always know this, but it is good to ask the customer: "What are your thoughts about resolving this situation?" Sometimes, we talk so much in our own heads about what we think the other person is thinking, and we forget to ask. So ask them: "How do you see us working together on this?"

6. **Consequences.** What are the consequences for you of winning or losing this situation? What are the consequences for your customer and for you? Put yourself in your customer's shoes. If he or she bought a service or a product that is not fulfilling his or her expectations, then the customer feels bad. Your customer just wants your help to resolve the situation. Most likely your customer doesn't want to go to the trouble of finding another vendor. Your customer bought from you and wants to stay with you—the consequence of not finding a resolution is usually bad for both parties. Both people end up feeling angry, annoyed, and frustrated. So do your best to maintain a great attitude—I promise, with good intentions, you will overcome any difficult situation.

7. **Power.** Where is the power in the relationship? Who controls it? Who stands to lose the most if agreement isn't reached? In *Super Service* terms, your customer has the power to accept the solution or not, and you have the power to maintain your great attitude and help find a solution. You always have the power over your attitude. It is not always easy, but it is always in your hands. Don't fall into the trap of feeling that your customers have all the power. You *always* have power over your choice—animal brain or human brain. When you operate from your human brain, you are able to accept, enjoy, and find solutions.

8. **Possible solutions.** Based on all of the considerations, what possible compromises might there be? Sometimes, you can't deliver what the customer wants. But knowing what you can and cannot provide is important in being able to provide *Super Service*. Always remember, your attitude is number one in helping to provide solutions.

▼

KEY POINT

Reaching agreement is about you wanting to reach agreement. Your customers know that you have the attitude that says, "I will help you resolve this situation."

Working with Diversity, Not against It

To reach agreement, we must be of one mind with the customer. How do we do that? We must operate from our human brain instead of our animal brain. If two people are communicating from their animal brain, it is a no-win situation. It results in arguments, confrontation, and frustration.

If just one person can switch their brain to be in their human brain, they are able to see the situation differently—they will look for solutions, ways to reach agreement, and behave as an evolved human being instead of someone who just wants to be right no matter what.

Wanting to reach agreement means we want peace more than we want combat. We want harmony more than we want arguments. Again, it doesn't mean we lie down and take whatever the customer wants to throw at us. It simply means we want agreement.

It is no different from being with a customer who has different opinions. We tell the customer: "I can see why you feel that way, and another way to look at it is . . ." or "If this problem keeps happening, maybe we should look at it from a different point of view."

Looking for the Win-Win Solution

Of course, there are always customers who are looking for a freebie; they try to get a replacement product, even when they have obviously been abusing the original. How you deal with that depends on:

- Company policy
- Whether the customer needs training on product use
- The costs involved (actual cost, goodwill)

We've heard some customer service advocates say, "It is a bad idea to give super service to every customer—that we must not treat all customers alike, because all customers are not alike. Some are loyal and put all their trust in us. Others are indifferent, and spend most of their money elsewhere."

We do not believe in this type of thinking—we believe every human being deserves to be treated with super service, and heer's why:

1. *Super Service* is about you being the best that you can be, because when you are being the best, you get to experience yourself at your best rather than at your worst. We want you to go home at the end of the day, feeling great.
2. The least profitable customers today, may become your most profitable tomorrow. None of us have a crystal ball, we don't know the future—so why not treat every customer as unique and special; that one customer may become your greatest asset
3. When you are being a customer, you want to be treated as unique and special—so why not treat others' how you want to be treated yourself? You don't want people judging whether you have the money to be a profitable customer or not and then serving you based on that judgement—you want to get super service no matter what.

Super Service is about seeking harmony and balance with your customers. Reaching agreement is not a battle of power. Many of us are raised to be competitive, to fight, to win, and be first. We've all heard the coach say: "Winning is not the most important thing; it's the only thing!"

We all have the impulse to win; the problem is that if there is a winner, there must be a loser. If someone comes first, someone else must come last. If the customer wins, you lose. Or if you win, the customer loses.

It doesn't have to be this way in *Super Service*. If you operate from your human brain, you win no matter what. The human brain wants peace, love, and harmony. It wants you to be happy, to live a fulfilled and happy life—reaching agreement is just an extension of that.

If we turn these competitive urges into complementary urges, we all get what we need. The inner battles stop. The conflict stops. The *selfish* chatter of "me, me, me" stops. Reaching agreement is making it right for *everyone* concerned. The statement, "Do unto others as you would have them do unto you," becomes a living action, and your heart figuratively opens.

But we are not advocating giving away the whole shop. This is a business book, and the most profitable business is a direct result of *Super Service*. Do you know the costs involved in your solutions? You should! *Super Service* is about reaching agreements in the most profitable way. Can you answer the following questions?

1. How much does your product or service cost to repair?
2. How much does your product or service cost to replace?
3. How important are customers to your company?
4. Do certain customers deserve special treatment?
5. How loyal are your customers?
6. What is the lifetime value of one of your customers?

Every customer is different. Some customers need a huge amount of attention, and other customers don't want to hear from you, until they have a problem. As a service provider trying to solve customer problems, you need to be looking for the most cost effective ways to satisfy your customers. Your job is to help your company make a profit and to do it in the most harmonious way for all concerned. Sometimes serving a customer profitably is not possible and you have to turn away the business.

We once decided that we did not want to do business with a particular customer. Why? We had done one project a year for the past two years, we had never made a profit, and the job always turned out to be a nightmare. From the get-go, we were "nickeled-and-dimed" to death. There was no profit margin, and the aggravation for our staff was too much for the job to be worthwhile. The projects took a lot of energy, the person in charge was very difficult to deal with, and—the bottom line—we had to wait over five months for our invoice to be paid. Sometimes it is better to walk away from "bad" business than to be depleted of energy and profit.

We hope we have made it clear that *Super Service* is not about throwing ourselves at the feet of every customer. We are not promoting the subservient characters out of Charles Dickens, tugging on our forelock with cap in hand! What we are saying is to switch to your human brain—and use reason, objectivity, and common sense.

How to Seek Win-Win Solutions

There are many books about negotiating. We ask that you move beyond the accepted concept and place your mind at a higher level—we could even say a more enlightened level. *Super Service* is about achieving harmony by becoming totally straightforward and honest with ourselves. We strive to purify our thoughts and attitudes and create a working environment that promotes openness, kindness, and wise communication. This objective is hard to achieve if we are thinking of negotiation tactics and counter-tactics.

How about turning the negotiating concept inside out and upside down? What about listening to what your customers really need and want? What about suspending your own judgments and treating customers (who may be strangers or even people you dislike) as if they are beloved relatives who have a serious problem? Imagine customers are beloved relatives. How would you help them?

You would probably want them to be happy, satisfied, and content. You would *really* listen to the issues and want to help resolve them. If they had a grievance, you would actually understand why they are hurting. You would show compassion and empathy because they are close to you. Why not treat your customers this way?

Try it tomorrow at work. Empty your mind and be everything you can be for the other person. And don't worry that your mind will remain empty; as soon as the person stops talking, your mind will be as full as ever! And when the customer has gone, you will start talking to yourself again as usual!

"Did I really empty my mind for him?"
"Did I have the desire to serve like the book said?"

"Was I judgmental?"
"Was I sincere about his problem?"

Build on the Customer's Proposal

Have you ever been in a conversation that seems to flow beautifully and you don't know why? It's often because that person is mirroring something that we like in ourselves. It is the same when we listen to a speaker. If he or she is saying something that we agree with, we nod our heads in agreement, as if we are the ones up there saying it!

When customers propose something, it's not a good idea to say, "No, we have to do it this way." Instead, we should build on their proposal. Here are some guidelines:

1. Explain to the customer why you offered the solution and how it will help the situation.
2. Ask questions to gain a better understanding of the situation.
3. Check your understanding by explaining the problem in your own words.
4. Incorporate the customer's ideas into your solution.
5. Build and communicate on the joint ideas.

Be Creative

We all have huge amounts of creativity; some people are more open to using it than others. Creativity means being open to new ideas. Sometimes, we think that creativity in business is different from creativity in the artist's studio. Not so. Creativity is creativity wherever it is applied.

If you get into a slump, it becomes visible to everyone around you; be creative in finding your way out, and ask yourself the following questions:

1. What worked in the past?
2. What is not working now?
3. What can I do differently?
4. What resources do I have?

Have fun getting out of your rut:

1. Dress differently for a day. (It doesn't need to be drastic. For example, if you normally wear black, then wear red.)

2. Style your hair differently and see how it makes you feel.
3. Find a good joke to tell everyone.
4. Eat different food from what you would normally choose.
5. Cut out the coffee and find a new way to wake up.

Promises

Don't overpromise and underperform. If you give a false set of expectations for yourself or for your company, you may not be able to meet them down the road. It is misleading to:

1. Give the impression that the product will be repaired at no cost, if in fact that is not the truth.
2. Allow customers to think their equipment will be repaired much sooner than is possible, just to calm them down.

Here are some ways to calm customers down, without misleading them or overpromising:

1. "You do not have coverage for this repair. I can provide a service contract that will take only two days to put through and will benefit you for one year. The cost for that is $_____. May I do this for you?"
2. "Ms. Jones, I cannot schedule the service call until Wednesday morning. There are no time slots until then. However, I am putting you down for first priority if there is a cancellation. How does that sound?"
3. "I certainly understand why you need a copy of the invoice today, Mr. Smith; unfortunately, the report doesn't come out until tomorrow. I will get the request in right away to be processed first, so I can call you by 10 o'clock tomorrow morning. Will that be satisfactory?"

How to Not Give Away the Shop

Here's something to keep in mind: *You do not have to do whatever the customer suggests.*
Here are two questions that will help you make the right decision:

1. Does the customer's proposal truly answer his or her needs?
2. Will it satisfy and resolve the issue?

The best proposal is the one that keeps both parties in business.

Here are some suggestions on how to *not* give away the shop, and yet still honor your own feelings. One is to use humor:

The customer says, "I want a new product. This one doesn't work; you have to replace it for free!"

Say, "I understand how you feel, but this product has been warrantied to last at least six years. Why don't we service it and replace some of the parts and save you a lot of money!"

This way, you have let the customer know that whatever happens, it is going to cost something to replace the parts. You are looking at the customer as if you are standing side by side on the same side of the fence, instead of on opposite sides feeling ill will toward each other.

You can exceed customer expectations without giving something away: Ask an extra question, give an extra smile, or respond to the problem promptly.

CHECK-IN

The task is to use phrases that show the customer you understand where they are coming from. Here is the clue: Since every action is preceded by a thought, we have to think good thoughts before we speak. Here are a few examples:

Think: **We are on the same side of the fence.**
Say: "I like your idea about . . ."

Think: **We want the same thing.**
Say: "We can work with your suggestion to . . ."

Think: **I want the best for both.**
Say: "From my experience I think your best option is . . ."

Think: **One small step is all it takes.**
Say: "I like your idea, and perhaps we can also . . ."

ACTION

After you have had some practice thinking good thoughts, you are now ready to speak. In your upcoming interactions with customers, speak from a place of good intention.

Note: Difficulties do not disappear; they are a part of life, especially in customer care. How we react to the difficulties makes the difference. Think good thoughts. Speak with wisdom and you will make the difference.

1. Choose one of the examples from the check-in on the previous page.
2. Copy the example in bold red pen on a piece of 8½ by 11-inch paper.
3. Pin the paper where you can see it.
4. Refer to it throughout the day as a reminder.

Chapter 7

CUSTOMER SERVICE KEY 5

Check Understanding

When you explain to customers *how* their service needs
will be met by your organization, they feel in control.

Here is how one of our clients, who participated in our *Super Service* workshop, answered the following three questions:

Carolina—Baxter Americas Services, Intercompany Supervisor
1. **As a customer, what do you want?**
   "I want quality, good customer service at the store, and a fair price."
2. **As a customer, what do you feel stops you from getting what you want?**
   "Definitely poor customer service. I just walk out of the store."
3. **In your experience, what do customer service people do best?**
   "Talk about options and provide relevant advice."

Here is how a subscriber to our newsletter at www.winnersattitude.com answered the following three questions:

Elizabeth—Enterprise Data Management, Director, Program Management
1. **As a customer, what do you want?**
   "The attention of the person I am dealing with."
2. **As a customer, what do you feel stops you from getting what you want?**
   "When people don't listen."
3. **In your experience, what do customer service people do best?**
   "Listen."

Your Energy Is Key

As you read this chapter, you will discover phrases to use and phrases *not* to use. You will learn steps and guidelines that will help make sure you are on the same page with your customer. But, before we tell you what these things are, we want to emphasize the importance of your energy—because your energy will either make or break a relationship. And we are talking about all of your relationships: customers, coworkers, friends, and family. If you do not check your level of energy, and tweak it to make sure it is in alignment with what you want to happen—it doesn't matter what skills, tools, and phrases you use—nothing will work.

Aligning your energy with what you want to happen is about being awake and conscious of the fact that *you* are the one making things happen. That you are the key to having successful relationships. If you are feeling grumpy, unhappy, and without passion, optimism, or joy, then that is the energy you are sending out. The energy that you send out is like a magnet. It attracts and draws the same kind of energy back to you. You've heard the saying, "misery loves company," well there's truth in that; people who are miserable seek out other people who are miserable so they can discuss how bad their lives are.

If you want to be happy, seek out successful, happy people. If your coworkers are miserable and hate their job, be the one who makes the change. Talk about the good parts of your job. View customers as human beings that you are helping.

Many people live their lives without even knowing, caring, or being aware of the kind of energy they are giving off. If they are feeling down, they will blame everyone else for their bad mood. If they are feeling up, they won't realize that they are the ones allowing it to happen.

When you wake up every morning and become aware of your energy; and if you want to have a great and wonderful life where you become a positive influence in the world, you will start to attune yourself to positive energy. You will listen to the news to understand what is going on in the world, but you will not get pulled in and be affected by it. You will not listen and become pulled in and be fearful, angry, or full of hate; you will listen and then you will let it go. You will listen to upbeat music that fills your spirit with joy. You will seek out people who are happy. You will search for the good things in people instead of looking for the bad. You will be a seeker of solutions instead of a seeker of problems.

▼

KEY POINT

Every morning, decide what kind of energy you want to have for the day. Do you feel tired? Then ask for energy that will replenish and lift you up. Direct your attention to things, people, and situations that make you feel good. Don't turn on the news. Avoid people who are miserable. Instead, listen to some upbeat music. Call a friend who has a positive and optimistic attitude.

You will make sure that you live a life that restores your good spirits, instead of living a life that drains you of your good spirits. Some of you may read this and say, "Yes, but with my job, I can't stay happy. My customers have bad energy and they pull me down." Like this one person who wrote a review about the first edition of *Super Service* on Amazon.com said:

> *"Just try getting screamed at, cursed at, things hurled at you, and called all kinds of different names from an irate customer. Also try wading through the asinine company policies that tie your hands and keep you from helping the customer the way they deserve. Along with a lower-than-you-can-live-off salary, and you have the average customer service rep and what we have to deal with every day."*

It's interesting to read reviews about *Super Service*. Most of them are excellent, but this one is great because it paints the very worst picture of what one person's experience is of being a customer service provider or rep. This person is practically begging for irate customers to come along because that is the kind of energy that he or she is sending out. Customers scream, hurl things, and curse! Yes, I know that some customers do that, but most do not. Most customers just want what they want—great service, solutions, and products that do what they say they will do.

If you work for a company that ties your hands with policies, then it is your job to be the best that you can be and find solutions that work, which allow your company to make a profit and give the customer a quality product at the same time. If you work for a company that is not providing quality service or products, then maybe you need to think about working somewhere else. You don't have to stay in a job that makes you feel bad; there are plenty of companies who want to provide great customer service—bottom line for you, it is always your choice.

Here's how another reviewer responded to the customer service rep who deals with mostly negative customers:

> *". . . Every day is a job interview and every customer, an interviewer. It's a frame of mind; customer service people have chosen their career and with that, comes tremendous responsibility. Sometimes they are underpaid but so are teachers, cops, firemen, and a slew of others."*

I've noticed that most customer service providers or reps are amazing. They're on the ball, they answer questions, and they want to do a great job. They have great energy and they transmit it to their customers. And the most amazing thing is that it's a choice—your choice. Be great, do your best, expect great things, and great things will come to you!

▼

KEY POINT

When you check understanding, the first thing you must check is yourself. How is your energy? What kind of "vibe" are you sending out? What opportunities can you see that will uplift your spirit and allow you to enjoy your life?

When you check understanding with your customers you give them an opportunity to confirm that your solution meets their needs. *It does not mean restating the problem.* It means restating the steps of the solution in terms of cost, time, and service steps.

Here are the steps:

1. Make sure the customers understand the solution you have offered them.
2. Be prepared for customer input.
3. Verify the facts.
4. Check for agreement of plan.
5. Accept responsibility.
6. End on a positive note.

Unfortunately, these steps don't always go easily.

What the Customer Needs to Know

She's a man-hater! This was a problem that came up during a brainstorming session we were facilitating with a group of high-tech service providers. They told us that after many attempts, their customer would still not give them the correct information they needed to successfully do their job. It had escalated to such a point that the project had come to a halt. The brainstorming session would help, but a lot of venting went on first. "She doesn't want help! She won't give us access to the users! We can't implement the development stage. She's a control freak! She's chemically imbalanced!" The problem had become very personal, and the service providers were now highly charged and emotional.

We brainstormed the solutions: communicate effectively, educate the customer on the various steps, ask for input—solutions from the customer. But they kept going back to the problems—even when we had moved on to the solutions. They had lost all objectivity. The customer had become such a nightmare that they *wanted* to "lose her!"

"We're halfway through. We've made a good profit so far; we could hand it off to another group to finish!"

What had gone so wrong that it had come to this? When we talked about it further, we discovered that they had not *understood the customer's needs*. Their customer had been "burned" in the recent past, and our service providers didn't realize that her experience had affected her responses.

They had not addressed what their customer needed to know:

1. **Time.** How long was the project going to take?
2. **Target.** What will the outcome look like?
3. **Budget.** How much will it cost?
4. **Benefit.** Why are we doing the project?

Without a well-stated goal and without "checking understanding," our service providers were having a difficult time going back to their customer and saying:

"This is what we said we would do, in this amount of time, for this amount of money, for this benefit. We're now here. We've spent this amount, and we're nowhere near completion."

For a large project with your customer, you must have a well-defined goal and sign-off. Then, when the customer wants changes, you can say with hand on heart: "Sure we can do that; let's take a look at how that will impact the budget and deadline of the project."

In our brainstorming session, our customer service providers decided to talk to their customer about the project plan and, if possible, redefine the goals and tasks. By concentrating on the project plan, they could return objectivity to the situation. They could start working together *with* their customer instead of waging war.

Other service providers in this workshop talked about how one of their customers didn't want to pay the invoice: "They say we haven't done enough work to justify our costs!" This is another good reason for putting together a project plan and writing down all the tasks, subtasks, and even sub-subtasks. We need to see what we're getting for our money, and customers typically don't know all the work that goes into a product or a service.

Do you? Are you fully aware of all the tasks that you perform? Often we are so used to doing our job, we are unaware of how much time it takes to do certain tasks.

Tasks = Time = Money

After you have written a goal for a large project, brainstorm with a colleague all of the tasks necessary to bring it to completion. Itemizing the tasks helps your customer understand the size of the project and also where the money is going.

Customers' needs are not hard to understand. What do you want? What do your customers want? Underneath everything, we all want the same things: security, love, and human kindness. We all want to feel we made a good deal, that we didn't get "screwed." We need to know that if we paid money for something, it will work and, if it doesn't work, it will get replaced (as long as we haven't abused it and it is still under warranty!).

Standard Operating Procedure

You, me, your customers, your boss, your peers, and your colleagues all have standard operating procedures (SOPs)—the habits we have learned. The problem is we are usually too asleep to notice that we are using them.

What is your standard operating procedure? How do you react when the chips are down? Are you a giver or a taker?

You've probably heard of the fight-or-flight syndrome. If we get into trouble, either we stand and fight or we flee. Do you know what your reaction is? Become aware of it. Do you like an argument? Do you enjoy a battle? Or do you walk away? Drive off? Steer clear?

Learning how to handle your own problems will help you to understand other people's problems because you will recognize them. There are four stages to this learning:

1. Awareness
2. Awkwardness
3. Skill
4. Habit

In the **awareness** stage you become aware that you need or want to learn something different. Let's say that your standard operating procedure when dealing with customers is to be very judgmental. The first step is to know and recognize that you are judgmental.

You will know if you have this trait by just one thing: When you first meet customers, do you judge their clothes, how they speak, how they hold themselves, etc.? Or do you let all appearances fall away and see them simply as human beings?

The second stage is **awkwardness.** This occurs, for example, when you become aware of being judgmental and you decide not to be. Changing will be very awkward for you at first. Your SOP will want to put your customer into a "box," because that seems easier to deal with.

As another example, if your standard operating procedure is to gossip and you have become aware of this, go through the awkward stage of not being a gossip. Zip your mouth.

This takes you to the third stage: **skill.** It takes skill not to be a gossip! It means that you have to be in the present moment. If you enjoy what is happening right now—this very moment—you will come to realize there is no point in gossiping or being judgmental. There is no good in any of the other standard operating procedures that your mind has programmed for you.

This brings us to the fourth stage: turning a new skill into a **habit.** Don't fall asleep and let yourself go to default. Listen to yourself. Be aware of what you are saying and what action you are taking. Eventually, you will form the habit of being awake in your life. This is an important concept—to be awake. Where is your true self? We all have the same needs and wants and urges. Follow someone who is awake and don't be concerned about people liking you all the time. Do and say what you know is right.

Make your life something wonderful. Take time with people. If you are given a rotten job to do, do it as well as you can. Become a shining example for yourself and others. Light up your world! Light up your customers!

Manage Customer Expectations

Tell your customers what to expect. If we know what is going to happen, we feel in control. When we don't know what is going to happen, we feel as though we are spinning out of control with no idea where we're going to land.

If your plan is to hand over the customer's problem to the billing department, be sure to tell the customer and the billing department. Tell customers they don't have to re-explain everything, that you have done it for them, and that they should contact you again if they experience any problems. If the customer's problem means bringing in a third party or even another company, explain the "why-when-how."

However, as we have said before, you don't want to give away the entire shop. You are part of a business. Your job is to help your company grow profitably. Look at the two words: profit and loss! "Profit" has a glow to it, a life. "Loss" is something to be bereaved. You want to be profitable and to do so for the best of all concerned.

If you can help make your customers profitable, you are providing a wonderful service. Take a moment to write a list of everything about your product or service that will help your customers be profitable. Think in terms of saving them time or money, although the profitability can also be in the "feel-good" or "reaching-a-goal" department.

I HELP MY CUSTOMERS BE PROFITABLE BY:

1. _____

2. _____

3. _____

4. _____

Being *with* the Customer

Are you *with* the customers when you are with them? We often "brush" people off just because they don't fit into our image. That sounds harsh, doesn't it? Yet every time we dismiss people without finding out who they are, we are saying that they may as well *not* exist.

We all have a list of people whom we want to dismiss. Some think the elderly have nothing to offer. Others may think children are too noisy or that teenagers are undisciplined. The list goes on and on.

Become self-aware and start living! *Super Service* never stops! It is there with you all the time in and out of the office, at the department store, at the agency, in the hospice, the hospital or in the salon, wherever it is that you work. *Super Service* is not something you can turn on and off . . . it's who you are.

We are not saying that you have to spend all your time listening to a customer's personal problems or doing everything for one particular customer. "Being with a customer" means simply being present to help if we can, to extend a helping hand when we can, and to light up somebody's world with a smile.

Does this sound too simple—as if this is not about your job? Do you think your work is so stressful that you don't have time for the "people stuff"? The problem is that people are everything. We are social animals, in case you hadn't noticed.

In one of our project management courses, we discussed PERT charts, GANTT charts, work breakdown structures, crash path analysis, and task analysis worksheets. In the end, however, the most difficult thing to analyze was the people.

Yet, it is so simple. We all have needs. We all have the same needs. Therefore, personalize your service. Pledge to help. Be honest. Be open to new information from your customer. Even when you have an action plan in mind, and after you have reached agreement about how the problem should be solved, your customer may still have input. Be prepared to listen. Maintain the desire to serve.

Who is the most important person to you? *You* are! Customers are no different. They are the most important people to themselves. *Super Service* requires that you become *no thing* so that you can become *every thing* for your customer.

PHRASES TO AVOID

"I'll try."
"I'll try."
"I'll try."
"I'll try."

If you say "I'll try," the other person will think, "Yes, but will you?" If someone says, "I'll try to meet you at 9:00," do you really expect them to be there at 9:00? No, because they've already built in a big no. Most likely they will be late and have some excuse like the traffic, or the meeting went on longer than I expected. We tend to put up a lot of smokescreens when we talk to customers:

"I'll try to do that!"
"I'll try and make the meeting!"
"I'll try my best to get it finished."

These phrases do *not* inspire confidence. They do *not* tell the customer, "It will be done!"

PHRASES TO USE

"I will."
"I will."
"I will."
"I will."

When we say "I will," we are saying that something will be done. It's about committing to do something instead of committing to not doing it. If you want to complete something, you just need to work backwards: "This is the goal, what steps do I need to take to reach there?" or, "I said I would arrive at 9:00, what do I need to do to get ready and how much time will it take—okay, so if I want to be on time, I need to start getting ready at 8:00!" Now comes the integrity part:

Do you do what you say you are going to do?
Do you ever not do what you say you are going to do?
Do you sometimes do what you say if you feel in the right mood?

If you say you will do something for your customer, you *must* do it! If you do not think you can do something, you must say that you cannot do it! If you say you will try to do something, you are saying that it probably won't happen.

"I will send your request to . . ."
"I will talk to my manager . . ."
"I will get a service engineer out tomorrow . . ."
"I will take this to accounts payable . . ."

Become a person of integrity. Do what you say you will do.

CHECK-IN

Pin up this checklist where you can see it to remind you of the steps involved in checking understanding.

1. **Make sure the customer understands what you intend to do.** "So, to clarify, the service engineer will arrive on Monday.the 28th between 9 a.m. and 1 p.m.
2. **Be prepared for customer input.**
3. **Check notes.** This is your last chance to verify facts.
4. **Check for agreement of plan.** "Will these steps meet your needs?"
5. **Accept responsibility.** "Call me if there are any further issues."
6. **End on a positive note.** "I'm glad it worked out."

ACTION

Use your check-in list with the six steps during the next week. Work on checking understanding with all your customers. For one morning only, ask yourself the following questions:

1. Did I use the steps with my customers?
2. Do my customers understand how much my product or service or repair is going to cost, and how long it will take?
3. Am I giving my customers the understanding they need?

Obtaining customer understanding is much easier before the event than after.

Chapter 8

CUSTOMER SERVICE KEY 6

Take Action

Taking action not only helps you and the person
you are helping, it leads you to enlightenment.

Here is how one of our clients, who participated in our *Super Service* workshop, answered the following three questions:

Laura—GE Commercial Finance, Lean Leader
1. **As a customer, what do you want?**
   "I want someone that will listen and deliver based on my needs."
2. **As a customer, what do you feel stops you from getting what you want?**
   "Rep's personal agenda doesn't align with my needs. Perhaps it's a business metric (close the call in 'X' seconds . . .), only 'hear' part of the need, etc."
3. **In your experience, what do customer service people do best?**
   "The really good ones make a personal connection."

Here is how a subscriber to our newsletter at www.winnersattitude.com. answered the following three questions:

Dinah—Advanced Tower Services, Warehouse
1. **As a customer, what do you want?**
   "Friendly, accurate service."
2. **As a customer, what stops you from getting what you want?**
   "The 'I am just here for the dollars' attitude, and no pride in a job well done."
3. **In your experience, what do customer service people do best?**
   "Anticipate needs."

The IKTA Disease

When you take action, don't do it from the "**I K**now **T**hat **A**lready" place. We call this the IKTA disease. If you think you already know something, then you will stop looking, listening, and learning. It is like taking a walk in the forest. If you think you already know what a tree is, what a leaf is, and what the sky is, then you will stop looking and you will miss thousands of opportunities to learn something new.

That is how boredom sets in. People stop looking. They stop looking at their friends and family the way they did when they first met, and they stop seeing how amazing they are. When you were first in love with someone, you wanted to know all about them; you were interested and you wanted to listen. But once you think you know that person, you stop looking, you stop asking questions, and you stop listening. Then you maybe start seeing all the things that are wrong with that person.

▼

KEY POINT

Don't let the IKTA disease take over. When you label things, you stop looking. You think you already know it and that there is nothing else to learn.

A good saying to remember is, "You only see what you are looking for." When you look for things to go wrong, that's what you will see. When you look for problems, that's what you will see. So your homework for the next week, and for the rest of your life, is to look for the good. Look for the good in your customers, in your family, in your friends, in your coworkers, and in your managers and bosses. Look for what is good and you will see what is good. See what is good, and good things will happen to you.

▼

KEY POINT

You see what you are looking for. When you look for goodness in people that is what you will see. And when you see goodness that is what will come into your life.

Feed people with praise for things that they are doing well, and they will do more good things. We love to be told that we have done a good job. Customers love to be told thank you:

"Thank you for calling today."
"Thank you for bringing this problem to my attention."
"Thank you for your business."

Nothing can ever be accomplished by wishing or talking, only ACTION makes things happen. It's time to get in motion and start achieving your goals. Actions speak louder than words. We all know the people in our lives whom we can depend on and those we cannot—who keeps their word and who doesn't. The strange thing is that often the people who don't keep their word speak longer and louder than those who do!

Have you noticed how some people jump into projects only to get burned out halfway through? It's easy to do and there are many reasons:

1. **Boredom**. The project loses its sparkle.
2. **Complexity**. It is harder than we thought.
3. **Resources**. We haven't got the people or equipment.
4. **Money**. We have run out of cash.
5. **Time**. It is taking too long.

You can probably come up with a lot more reasons why projects don't get finished.

However, there is a simple remedy—so simple you may not want to hear it. Here it is: *Don't start something you can't finish!*

What does that mean? It means take a look at your life. How do you manage it? Do you have too many things on your plate at once? If so, delegate or finish what you have before taking on anything else. If your boss asks you to take on more, say, "Does this take priority over projects 3, 4, and 5? Or do you want me to finish those first?"

Pointing out that you have other projects that need completing is not rude. Yes, it is rude if you say it in a nasty or mean way, but if you simply state what you have going on, you are being pro-active—you are letting people know that you have a lot of work to do and if something else is being added, then you need to prioritize.

Turning Negatives into Positives

Are you using too many negative words? Do you hear yourself saying every day: "I'm tired," "I can't do this," "I hate this," or "I'm bored!"? Maybe you need to change the CD.

The beliefs you have about yourself are extremely powerful because they become what other people see in you. If you go around moaning, that is what people hear. Your chant makes you the person you are!

Think about the unhappy people in your life. What words do they use? If you close your eyes for a moment and visualize their faces in front of you, they probably look sad and, if you listen carefully, you will hear them repeating over and over their sad words.

If you are like that, what can you do? First you have to be *aware*! What do you say? How do you say it? Listen to the words that seem to pop out of your mouth without your even knowing. Then comes the awkward part; when you hear the words pop out, you have to say the opposite: instead of "I'm bored," say "That's not really true, I'm really very content!"

We hope that you don't use negative words with your customers. (*Remember: "My customer is anyone who is not me!"*) Whomever you are talking with is your customer. Your words are like seeds; they scatter and fall all over your world. People hear them and learn what kind of person you are. Change your words and you will change your life. Instead of "I can't do numbers," say "I'm getting better at numbers!"

In the following list, pick out one or two negative phrases that you recognize yourself as saying. Start using the positive affirmations instead:

Instead of . . .	**Use . . .**
"I hate myself."	"I love myself."
"I'm bored."	"I'm content!"
"It'll never happen."	"It will happen!"
"Nothing works out for me."	"Everything works out for me!"
"I never get what I want."	"I get everything I want!"
"My life is horrible."	"My life is great!"
"My customers are all difficult."	"My customers are all great!"
"I can't find happiness."	"I have happiness!"
"I'm not fulfilled."	"I am fulfilled."

It cannot be stressed enough that thought precedes action. *Super Service* recommends that you become aware of your thoughts. If you have lots of negative thoughts, get rid of them by writing them down and then burning the paper. These thoughts are not meant to be seen by others. Then take action in something positive.

Here's an example. Some of us wake up in the morning feeling depressed. We don't know why; it just seems to happen, except we are in charge of our thoughts. What you think of as a horrible prospect—of another workday—can now become your greatest gift! You have the opportunity to change for the better! Replace a depressing thought with a good one:

"I hate my customers" *becomes* "I am going to do a great job for them!"
"I hate my job" *becomes* "I am going to learn everything I can in this job!"

If you change your thinking, you will change your actions.

Gandhi said, "How I live my life, that is my teaching." We are the same. If we profess peace in public and kick the cat in private, we are not fooling anyone but ourselves. If we then beat ourselves up because we kicked the cat, we are even trying to fool ourselves; but it won't work. Instead of taking your anger out on others, go for a walk, a run, do something that will activate your human brain instead of your animal brain.

Right Thought Comes before Right Action

Your customers want you to take action on their behalf. They come to you because they have nowhere else to go. If they could solve the problem themselves, they would. Think about your own experience as a customer. It takes time and effort to make a complaint or return defective merchandise. Most of us don't want the hassle. But think about the time when a service provider helped you—when you got more than you even imagined! Wasn't it fabulous? Didn't it restore your faith in human beings?

Why not be that person yourself? Why not restore faith in humankind? When you say you are going to take action, don't pass the buck; instead, make it happen! Become known as a person who gets the job done. And when you can't do a job, you say with hand on heart, "I can't do this right now. When I have some free time I will!"

Taking action not only helps you and the person you are helping, it leads you to enlightenment. You feel a sense of purity, a feeling that you are pure and that your heart is open.

When you take the right action, you wipe your internal slate clean from past mistakes. Your internal state of being feels cleaner, purer, and more blissful. Think about the number of people who get into a bad place with some addiction like alcohol, or drugs; when they wake up and realize what is happening, they are able to turn it around and begin to help others who have lost their way.

You have the choice. You can choose to beat yourself up or change your thoughts and take the right action. The "process" of your life makes you the person you are.

As an example, we were in an ice cream parlor recently and being served by someone who, in the words of the friend who was with us, "made the hair on my neck stand on end!" He was sulky and had a very bad attitude. Of course we made allowances. "Maybe he lost his mother!" "Maybe he has money problems." Yet the ice cream took on the flavor of the server. It didn't taste as good or as sweet as it could have. The grumpy demeanor of the server "poisoned" the ice cream! We left most of it and walked out.

We can do the same with our customers without even knowing it. We can go through the process exactly right: Use the right phrases, say the right things, produce the right solution, and ask at the end, "Is everything okay?"

Customers might reply, "Ah, yes, everything's great, thank you!" Yet, as they walk away, they're thinking, "I'm never going to use that place again!" The grumpy attitude is what people remember. We can try to cover it up with words, but it doesn't really help. The problem is that customers don't want to hear excuses. They want us to take the right action and, if we take the wrong action, they never forget.

In our lives, we can remarry the same type of person over and over again, go for the same kind of job over and over, or find ourselves repeatedly in the same troubled situations. All the while we wonder, "How on earth did this happen again?"

The reason: We forget! We forget the consequences from the last time we took that action. We forget that the last time we spoke to people that way, they got mad. Ultimately, we don't want to clearly see ourselves, because we are too fearful of what we might find! Yet when we take a clear look at ourselves, we are not nearly as bad as we think we are—and we can change!

Change is a strange thing. You may have heard the phrase, "A leopard can't change its spots." However, it seems to be a different thing when we are talking about a caterpillar. Caterpillars do change. They transform into butterflies.

Do we as human beings have the capacity to change? Absolutely and without a doubt! Just look around. You know people who have changed: alcoholics who have been on the wagon for decades, drug addicts who have reformed their lives, and on and on.

If you want to become the kind of person who can be relied on, who will complete tasks and be committed, you must first have the right thought:

"I commit myself to this task and I will see it through completion with a joy-filled heart!"

Is that too much for you? Then take out some of the words and just say, "I commit myself to a joy-filled heart!" Isn't that what you want? To be happy! To enjoy your life! Of course it is, and there is no better time to start than right now—by changing your attitude and taking the right action.

Behavior Is What Customers Remember

If you have listened to your customers and identified their needs, you are ready to carry out the action plan. This means taking action to ensure that the right steps are taken, by the right people, as fast as possible. Simply stated: It means doing what you said you would do!

You need to follow up with your customers, keeping them informed of any progress or delays. Many customers complain about a lack (particularly in large organizations) of communication between departments or employees. To reduce this cause of friction, make sure you let the right people know what they need to know. Keeping people informed before something happens is much easier than telling them after the event.

Often, the small tasks that we put off create the most problems, like answering our messages. We are tired; we don't want to return calls. We put things off until later, but it doesn't get any easier; it just gets later! So our suggestion is:

1. Act on messages as soon as you get them.
2. Respond to each voice mail and e-mail as soon as you receive it.
3. Put things back where you found them.
4. Keep people informed of any changes that affect them.

On the next page are six keys to taking action the right way. Incidentally, when you write your e-mail in all capital letters, it looks as though you are shouting. Also, keep follow-up guidelines short, simple, and to the point.

TAKE ACTION

1. **Give regular updates and progress reports.** Let customers know what is going on so they are prepared.
2. **Communicate delays promptly.** If customers know about delays, they can make changes in their schedules.
3. **State exactly what was done.** Without using technical terms or jargon, explain what was done and what steps you have taken.
4. **Give a personal reassurance to the customer.** Tell the customer that you have solved the problem.
5. **Help your customer to be proactive.** By providing information about preventive maintenance, you help yourself and your customer.
6. **Thank your customer.** As always, the customer has made an effort to bring the issue to your attention. It is much better to be told something is not working than for the customer to switch to the competition.

When the Company Is Used as an Excuse for Bad Action

Sometimes, it seems easy to blame the company for the problem:

"Oh, those people in service, they never do things on time!"
"I wish they'd get their act together in accounting!"
"It's sales, we've had lots of similar problems in the past."

When customers hear phrases like these, what do they think?

"This person has no loyalty to the company. It must not be such a great company if they hire people who talk this way!"
"I have no confidence in this person or the company."
"I'm glad this person doesn't work for me!"

When we moved offices, we had to have new telephones installed. The engineers didn't arrive when they were supposed to. We called and were told it would be six days before they could come out. Meanwhile, we were supposed to function without telephones! We got them to come out two days later.

When the engineer came, he said, "I only put the lines in, I'm not supposed to touch the phones!" The new telephones came with a 60-page booklet! We needed help to understand how to transfer calls, page other offices, etc. Finally, when the engineer realized the task ahead, he started to get mad—not at us, but at his telephone company. "I don't think those people in the office know what they're doing!" he said. "I think the salesperson sold you a phone system with too many bells and whistles! Do you really need all these functions?"

His reaction made us uncomfortable. Had we bought a telephone system that was too sophisticated for our needs? Could we rely on this person to do a good job?

Bad-mouthing your company is a "lose-lose" situation. If what you say is true, then do something about it. Talk to the people in accounting, service, or wherever the problem is. It is up to you to take pride in where you work.

We complained to the telephone company and got the installation charge taken off. We felt somewhat better, but we would still have preferred it not to have happened in the first place. Why?

1. We were out of contact with our customers for two days.
2. It was a hassle to solve the problem.
3. We had to lodge a complaint, which takes time and energy.

What happened next was also not good. When we got our bill, the installation charge had not been taken off. It took almost an entire day to track down the right person to take the charge off the bill. It took another amount of effort to explain what happened. It was a disaster in customer service follow-up.

On the next page are some guidelines that would help eliminate what happened to us.

GUIDELINES FOR CUSTOMER SERVICE FOLLOW-UP

1. **Confirm that the problem is resolved.** Once a problem is solved, the customer may not know it has been solved. Use phrases like, "I have taken care of the installation charge. It will not appear on your next statement. If you have any questions please call [*your name, phone number, or reference number*] as a contact."

2. **Verify satisfaction.** Find out if the solution meets the customer's needs and be prepared to accept a positive or negative response. For example, you could say, "I'm calling to follow up and make sure your invoice is correct. I hope your telephone system is working well for you now."

   Do not show disappointment or frustration if the customer says "no!" Keep your tone of voice steady and calm and find out what is wrong.

3. **Check for new problems and/or opportunities.** Sometimes, one solution brings up other problems or opportunities to do more business. So never be afraid to find out what is happening and how the customer feels.

As usual, there are phrases to use and phrases to avoid. Generally, they are fairly commonsense ones:

PHRASES TO AVOID

"It's usually an operator problem and not the product."

"I don't understand why you are still frustrated. I thought the problem was solved!"

"Have they been able to sort out your problem yet?"

PHRASES TO USE

"Let me make sure I have the right number: 6587, is that correct?"

"I'm adding your name to our database, so we can contact you when our new enhancements come out. Is that okay?"

"It was a pleasure working with you, and thank you for bringing your problem to our attention."

"Your account has been credited."

"Your system is now working correctly."

"Does this meet your needs?"

CHECK-IN

Think about all the ways you can improve on taking action. Add your personal action steps at the end of the following list:

1. Take initiative.
2. Be responsible.
3. Be willing to make decisions.
4. Use right thinking before acting.
5. Get input from the customer.
6. Listen for clues as to how the customer is feeling.
7. Develop a clear mental picture of the situation.
8. Use compassion when speaking the truth.
9. Remember we all want the same things.
10. Keep your tone quiet and peaceful.
11. Let your barriers down.
12. Have a desire to serve.
13. Clarify, verify, and check for mutual agreement on problems.
14. Communicate delays promptly.
15. Explain the action plan steps.
16. Reassure the customer that the solution has been accomplished.
17. Thank the customer.
18. Get the action plan done within the stated time frame.
19. Find other potential requirements.
20. _____
21. _____
22. _____
23. _____
24. _____

ACTION

On your next customer interaction, ask yourself the following question: How can I improve my follow-up actions so that I complete things in a responsible way?

- Once you have answered this question, you have moved into awareness.
- The next step is to push through awkwardness. In other words, it will feel awkward to bring new follow-up actions into your work routine until you feel comfortable with the skill.
- Keep using the skill until it becomes a habit. This is when you do the step without thinking. This is when you can pat yourself on the back and say, "I did it!"

Chapter 9

CUSTOMER SERVICE KEY 7

Build on Satisfaction

Added value means going the extra mile or beyond the call of duty.

Here is how two of our clients, who participated in our *Super Service* workshop, answered the following three questions:

Lecia—AO Smith, American Site Inspection Coordinator

1. **As a customer, what do you want?**

   "I need the ability to juggle many tasks every day. I am receiving assignments that need to be processed within five days from the receipt of them, which will include having to call contracted service providers to go and complete the paperwork."

2. **As a customer, what do you feel stops you from getting what you want?**

   "Sometimes, the service providers will accept the call but fail to remember to return the completed paperwork back to me; therefore, I have to make several follow-up calls or send reminder faxes. I will also have misdirected phone calls that I will have to address in order to keep our callers happy with our customer service. Sometimes, coworkers will not think for themselves. They will ask me a question that in the process they should realize that they are already solving their own question with the obvious solution. It creates distractions."

3. **In your experience, what do customer service people do best?**

   "We <u>listen</u> to someone complain about the product and realize that they are hoping in today's tough economic era that we can turn a bad situation into a better situation for them. We <u>explain</u> the company policies so that if we have to tell the customer no, they will understand why we are refusing their request. We <u>appreciate</u> the crazy caller antics because it reminds us how we should not act when we are not at work and we are receiving bad customer service somewhere else. I make sure to not voice my opinions at the top of my lungs for all to hear; I simply bring it to the correct manager's attention or I decide to not go back to a place that I find repulsive. "

Rick—Healthcare Financial Services, Marketing

1. **As a customer, what do you want?**

   "I do not care as much about what somebody knows until I know they care."

2. **As a customer, what do you feel stops you from getting what you want?**

   "Not articulating exactly what I am looking for and not having the 'salesperson' listening to my needs."

3. **In your experience, what do customer service people do best?**

   "Listen to my issue/problem/question:"

I was in a busy restaurant the other day, and the hostess took us to a table that was near the entrance. She apologized that it wasn't the greatest table, which is not great. You don't want to sow the seed in the customers' mind that they are not getting the best service, or the best seat, or the best product.

I said to her "No problem! This is a great table, we can people watch." And she said, "Yes, there are lots of crazy people coming in and out of here; in my business, I get to see them all." I smiled because she was sharing a joke, but I had the thought, "I didn't mean that I wanted to watch crazy people—I just meant I was people watching."

But the hostess was focused on watching crazy people, and sure enough, customers at the table next to us started to complain about the time it was taking for them to be served. Finally, the owner of the restaurant came out and had to talk to them for a long time, and even gave them a free meal.

So, we have to be careful what we say to customers. As a customer service provider, it is not good to think that the general public consists of a crazy bunch of people. If we start thinking that way, then that is what we will attract. Remember, "The Law of Attraction?" "That which is likened unto itself is drawn."

KEY POINT

The Law of Attraction says people's thoughts (both conscious and unconscious) dictate the reality of their lives.

"Added value" means thinking and expecting people to be great. It is like the 80/20 principle which came from Vilfredo Pareto, the Italian economist and sociologist, who noticed that 80 percent of Italy's wealth was owned by 20 percent of the population. It also applies to a variety of other situations, for example, we wear our 20 percent most-favored clothes about 80 percent of the time, and we spend 80 percent of the time with 20 percent of our acquaintances. If you apply the 80/20 rule to your customers from a positive perspective, you will think that 80 percent of them *are* great. If you think of it from a negative perspective, you will think that 80 percent of them *are not* great, and you are creating a difficult time for yourself.

Added value is about you thinking of your world, your life, your job, your relationships, and your customers as being amazing 80 percent of the time. Yes, you know that problems will happen, and that customers will be negative—but you only expect it to happen 20 percent of the time. You can deal with that easily. What you can't deal with is 80 percent problems and 20 percent solutions.

When you add value, you are viewing your situation from a positive point of view. You are able to find solutions because 80 percent of the time everything is going smoothly.

▼

KEY POINT

Consider the 80/20 rule; are you giving thanks 80 percent of the time, or are you complaining 80 percent of the time? Use your conscious effort to give thanks and remember your blessings 80 percent of the time.

Maybe it is because we are too slow to give thanks and too quick to complain that we see life as a struggle and difficult. It does not have to be that way if you would just get out of yourself and start to think about doing a kindness for your customer. Yes, maybe your customer is being really difficult, defensive, and even talking abusively, but you don't have to take it on board. You don't have to make it personal. You can think of your customer with kindness, with love even. Haven't you been in situations where you have been so angry you can't even think straight? Wouldn't you have loved to have just one person who accepted you as you were without being critical? You can do that. You can be that person who accepts and loves the difficult customer. You can help that customer just by not taking his or her actions and comments personally.

▼

KEY POINT

Be kind to yourself and to your customers. Don't take what they say personally. Be kind, compassionate, and loving. It will make you feel better.

Build on What Is Working

A psychiatrist friend once told us, "When clients come to me for self-improvement or counseling for a problem, I always ask them to tell me about a time when everything 'worked' really well for them. Then we build on that." It's the same with customers. Yes, we have to listen to the problems, but do we ever think to build on their satisfactions? Do we think to ask questions like:

"When it worked well, what was the best aspect?"
"Can you tell me about the best part of the product or service, and how that worked for you?"

When you are building on satisfaction, be sure to emphasize that you will work with customers to find a solution and that you want to make sure the solution will work well for them into the future. *Super Service* is what the customer *feels* when he or she has been dealt with in the right way—it is not always about giving more customer service, it's about giving the right service.

Values Process

One of the best ways to build satisfaction with your customers is to build it in your own life and in your job. One way to do this is to go through a "values process": simply identify what you personally value in your life and in your job. This discovery process will give you an opportunity to see your job as something that is personally important to you, and not simply as a way to pay your bills.

For example, if you enjoy creating great relationships with people, then you can acknowledge that part of your job: "I communicate with customers in an effective way and build great relationships." If part of your personal identity is to be of service, then you can say: "I am being of service in my job by helping people solve problems and find solutions."

▼

KEY POINT

Identify at least one way in which your job supports what you value in your life.

Be Helpful

Keep your customer informed of new and helpful data. In this high-tech world, products and services change daily. If software companies waited to release their product only when it had the final upgrade or enhancement, the product would never make it to the stores.

Correspondingly, customers could wait forever to buy the final software versions. So, as a *Super Service* provider, you can keep customers informed of new product enhancements and services. Here is an example:

> *"Just for your information, would you like to hear about the new enhancement for your system 300? I think it will help reduce the problems you've been experiencing."*

On the Front Line

Make your job your business. It makes no sense to be a *Super Service* provider if you don't take your job seriously.

Think of yourself as a business owner. After all, you are at the front line, liaising between the customer and your company. Take responsibility for your job and your customers. If you are waiting for the computer to access customer account information, ask the customer if he or she has been satisfied with prior orders. This may uncover "opportunities" to provide and sell additional services. No matter how good the product, if the service provider isn't doing a good job, the customer will not stick around, especially if competition is selling the same type of product or service.

Besides helping your company be successful, you get the feeling of achievement. If you lose this job, your skills are easily transferable because you are a valuable asset to any company. Added value means going the extra mile or beyond the call of duty, like this story we heard from Vodafone, one of our clients:

What do you do if the person you're talking to can't hear your voice? Sam had to address that problem when a deaf customer visited his tele-communications store in London, UK. Communicating with each other through written notes and questions, Sam decided right then that he wanted to learn sign language. The man was not in fact his customer. He'd come into the store because he was having problems with his mobile and he wanted to get the customer services number for a competive service provider. Looking at his phone, Sam noticed it didn't have a vibrating alert, which is clearly a vital feature for deaf users. By the end of their encounter Sam had converted the man to a new vibrating phone with his company. He'd also made the decision to teach himself how to sign. He began that night, picking up the basics by matching words on the evening news. After a month of doing that he bought some books, and within a year he was fluent.

During this time, the word was spreading among the local deaf population—someone in Sam's store knew sign language. When news reached the head of the regional deaf and dumb association they began to officially recommend the store to their members. This was important because the company's offer was not favored at that time among the deaf and mute community.

Sam has successfully marketed the company's products and services to the target audience by using their language. The store has 50 deaf customers who regularly drop in to look at new products or just to have a chat.

Many of them spend time there correcting any mistakes and teaching him new words, including the man who first inspired Sam's amazing story. Since teaching himself, Sam has begun giving lessons to two of his colleagues, meaning that there is always someone who can provide this unique service. In our business, and especially in retail, we spend a lot of time thinking about and using new ways of communicating. But Sam's passion for connecting with people goes way beyond technology. From that very first meeting, he has created unique customer experiences that make the people he is dealing with feel appreciated, confident, and inspired.

▼ KEY POINT

Identify three ways you can add value to your customer:

1. _____

2. _____

3. _____

CHECK-IN

Think back to yesterday and list your successes. List everything and anything: from not eating the chocolate donut, to helping a colleague find a document, to getting home early because it was your child's birthday.

Make the list of all your successes in the following spaces:

1. *I stayed late to finish a project.*

2. _____

3. _____

4. _____

5. _____

6. _____

7. _____

8. _____

9. _____

10. _____

11. _____

12. _____

13. _____

14. _____

15. _____

16. _____

17. _____

ACTION

Build on your successes. We all know and constantly beat ourselves up about our unsuccessful stuff. Now it is time to turn yourself inside out and see the good parts of yourself. Follow these steps:

1. Tomorrow, when you wake up in the morning, repeat to yourself, "Today I will build on my successes!"
2. Take just one of the successful actions that you listed, and build on it today. Each day pick a different one.
3. Know that by taking this action, you will move forward into recognizing that you are a successful person! You accomplish successful things in your life. You are awake to your successes and you build on them.

PART III

Advanced Customer Service Skills

Chapter 10

How to Handle an Unhappy Customer

It doesn't matter if customers are right or wrong. They need to air their complaints.

Here is how one of our clients, who participated in our *Super Service* workshop, answered the following three questions:

Salah—Vodafone, Engineering Manager

1. **As a customer, what do you want?**

   "I want to get my desired service literally as I described it in the fastest possible time."

2. **As a customer, what do you feel stops you from getting what you want?**

   "Several reasons:

   a. *Customer service didn't listen clearly to what I need*

   b. *Lazy and slow service providers*

   c. *Unreasonably expensive service providers*

   d. *Customer service didn't stick to their commitments."*

3. **In your experience, what do customer service people do best?**

   "Several good things I see from customer service people:

   a. *Being responsive and prompt*

   b. *Listen and understand carefully to what I need*

   c. *Communicate immediately when something happens*

   d. *Exceeding what they committed to do*

   e. *Price their service reasonably."*

Here is how a subscriber to our newsletter at www.winnersattitude.com answered the following three questions:

Eric—Ferguson Fire & Fabrication, Outside Sales

1. **As a customer, what do you want?**

   "I want to be cherished and taken care of. I want a product that fills a need, and I want to feel good about it."

2. **As a customer, what do you feel stops you from getting what you want?**

   "People's attitudes, society, backgrounds, and knowledge."

3. **In your experience, what do customer service people do best?**

   "Bend over backwards for their customers."

Communicate with Warmth

This is a story we were told by Vodafone, when we designed, developed, and facilitated six Performance Driver Programs. Connie is the manager of the 25-strong team of collections agents in the Netherlands. Her role is to make sure that the right policies are in place for customers who are in arrears. That includes ensuring that everyone knows how to have conversations with overdue customers.

In a fiercely competitive market, it is evermore important to keep the existing customer base happy. With that objective in mind the collections department decided that they should review the way they communicated. What that really meant was changing their way of thinking. For years, a customer in arrears had been seen as someone who was reluctant to pay their bill, a problem. The new goal was to focus on the person and not the immediate financial situation. They practiced how to communicate with more warmth, and how to give and receive criticism.

Taking the training back to the real world, they initially noticed an increase in the call time. People were spending longer on the phone as they had to listen to the customer and respond to their story. However results remained steady and targets were unchanged. Fewer customers were being disconnected, and longstanding customers in particular were agreeing on a lower number of installments to pay off arrears.

So, despite shifting the focus from results to people, the financial results have been very good. Connie believes it has been important to allow her team to feel connected to the results so they can see the impact their new style of working has been on the company.

The rewards haven't just been financial. The department is happier, and its image has been boosted internally. Seen in the past as strict and not friendly, they used to struggle to attract internal applications when vacancies came up. Since the new initiative this is no longer the case.

Questions about Angry Customers

Jeff facilitates hundreds of seminars worldwide. One particular series was called, "How to Handle Angry Customers." At the end of the series, participants had lots of questions about this topic. We felt they should be included in this chapter because they are so relevant to what customer service providers or reps really want to know. If you have any specific questions about anything to do with customer service, please contact us at coach@mjlearning.com. We will be happy to answer your questions. Here are some participants' questions.

Question: "How would you handle or deflect negative comments by customers or patients due to recent media coverage?"—*University Medical Center*

Answer: "A company that suffers bad press, for any reason, should immediately ensure that their customers are safe and not at risk from anything that the company product or service has knowingly or unknowingly created. They need to issue a press release and, in many cases, provide employees with a sample of answers to provide. These answers should provide honest, trustworthy remarks such as, 'Thank you for inquiring about the situation, we are working very hard to provide a solution; and to make sure this does not happen again. In fact we have (explain what the company has done to provide a solution). My name is Kent, and I would like to work with you to ensure that you receive the best possible customer service. How may I help you today?'"

Question: "We are a different type of business because we are not trying to gain customers for profit so there's no competition for our customers to go to. Are there specific steps for us to take when a customer isn't happy?" —*Southwest Water Company*

Answer: "It's the same formula for handling any customer who is not happy. First, perception is everything. Whether the customer is right or wrong, in his or her perception he or she is right and has been wronged. Bill Gates has said 'Your most unhappy customers are your greatest source of learning.' He is 100 percent correct! The only way we can improve is to constructively find out what is *not* working. Apologize sincerely and take responsibility for finding a solution. Stay calm and really listen to your customer. He or she is providing you with an invaluable learning tool. Throughout the conversation, take a moment now and then to summarize and repeat back to your customer what you feel is his or her issue. This promotes validation for the customer and a perception of being understood and valued. If needed, tell your customer that you will research further into the situation and provide follow-up as soon as possible."

Question: "Sometimes customers are very busy or hard to reach and I need reports from them to do my job better or to avoid future complaints or conflicts. How can I get the information I need without being pushy or aggressive?"—*International Paper*

Answer: "When I have this kind of situation, I use e-mails and telephone calls, and I come from a serving place. In other words, I am working for them and they are my boss. So for example I'd say—'I want to provide you with exactly what you want, because I appreciate your business. I know you're very busy and time is important to you; however, if you can get this information to me by this date, I will be able to. . . .' Then I tell them all the benefits they'll receive because of the action they take. It's the 'What's in it for me?' principle. I constantly use this method and ask myself why would they want to do this? How can my customer profit in this particular situation so that I can get what I need? All my e-mails and telephone calls come from this attitude. What is in it for the customer so that he or she will go ahead and give me the information I need? I give them incentive."

Question: "Do you have any tips for the first couple of seconds you are on a call with a customer to find out which of the four types of personality they are?" —*Oncology Nursing Society*

Answer: "It does come with practice but on the telephone we can pick up a lot of tonality. If the customer is *an amiable* he or she will speak in a quieter voice. An *expressive* is more exuberant; this customer will have more energy in his or her voice. A *driver* will be more specific and to the point. This customer will tend to be more clipped in his or her speech. An *analytical* will be more hesitant because he or she is constantly examining the conversation. Hopefully these descriptions will help. Also use the celebrity types. Donald Trump is a driver. Does your customer sound like him? Is she quiet, empathetic, and amiable like Barbara Walters? And as always, practice, practice, practice. Whatever personality style your customer falls into, the best thing you can do is mirror his or her style (unless they're angry or aggressive). Here are some tips to use with the different personality styles:

ANALYTICAL

- Slow down, listen.
- Be business-like; don't use small talk.
- Be accurate with facts and details.
- Prepare in advance.
- Use his or her experience and expertise.
- Explain rationale behind your decision.
- Explain how the situation will help.

DRIVER

- Use time efficiently.
- Stress results.
- Give options/ask what he or she wants.
- Be business-like; don't use small talk.
- Answer questions directly.
- Listen.
- Be willing to compromise

AMIABLE

- Slow down.
- Show personal interest.
- Give praise and strokes.
- Minimize power and authority.
- Ask for his or her help.
- Spell out changes that will affect him or her.
- Help him or her feel part of things.

EXPRESSIVE

- Keep it lively.
- Let him or her emote.
- Minimize detailed explanation.
- Stress exciting aspects.
- Give him or her a piece of the action.
- Give approval, recognize his or her abilities.
- Give incentives for the future.

Question: "How do you handle a customer who is using profanity and foul language?"— *Bell Communications*

Answer: "Hopefully, there are boundaries set up within your organization so that if your customer is using inappropriate language you know what to do—maybe call in your manager. If there isn't, you basically need to tell the customer that cursing or using profanity will not help solve their problem—'I hear your frustration level and I am committed to solving your problem and helping you with your concerns, unfortunately, we are going to have to stop the profanity because this is not helping.' You cool it down by being honest.

"If the customer continues to curse, say, 'I'm sorry but if you curse again, I will have to hang up and you can call back once you feel in a better place to talk.' Then, hang up immediately. Describe the situation in the call log and make a note of it in the customer's account. That way when the customer calls back an hour later, the next representative can be prepared for what may happen (a rude and angry customer); if the customer service representative isn't good with those situations, transfer the call to someone else.

"Don't get worked up if the customer is cursing at you. That won't solve anything and will just get you upset and stressed out more. Don't raise your voice—just stay calm and act like you normally do. If you can do that, you will be okay."

Question: "How can I defuse an angry customer who has already spoken to a few of our other facilities and given their story many times?" —*Walgreen*

Answer: "This is a valid concern; the initial call taker has had to get the information in order to see if he or she can resolve the problem or if he or she needs to pass it on. By the time the call is passed on, the customer is angry because he or she has had to repeat the information a few times. Of course, it is best if each person who takes the call tells the next customer service rep about the problem, but if this does not happen, then you need to handle their concerns and frustrations with honesty and truthfulness—'Mr./Ms. Jones, This is terrible and if I were in your situation I'd feel the same way. My name is _____ and I am the person who can actually resolve your problem right now.' Then get into the specific details—'I apologize that you have to repeat the information, but I do need just a few details. . . .' At the end of the call, thank the customer again for his or her time and patience—'Thank you for being such a great customer; I really appreciate your patience.'

"In this situation, you cannot pass the customer along to another CSR, you must take responsibility to resolve the situation yourself:

• Can you handle the situation on the spot?
• Can you offer a refund?
• Can you offer a replacement item?
• Can you offer a partial refund (or store credit) if the item cannot be returned?

"If there is no immediate resolution in sight, ask for the customer's home and work phone number, first and last name, and the best time to contact him or her. Let the customer know you will investigate the problem and get back to him or her within 24 hours. If you need more time, call the customer within that first 24 hours to let him or her know what you're doing to resolve the situation.

"I've also had the experience of an operator who has said to me I will connect you to someone who will resolve this but you will have to explain this again, so I was prepared.

"Allowing the customers to know what is happening is an excellent way of defusing the situation. Everyone likes to know the plan. There's nothing worse than not feeling in control of the call, especially if you are the customer. If we can erase some frustrations by telling the customer what's going to happen then do it."

Question: "What do you do if you've exhausted all of your options and solutions and the customer is still angry?" —*Sureco*

Answer: "There's an old saying, 'you can't win them all.' And consulting with many corporations, there are certain customers you don't actually want. Maybe this is the situation. All you can do is the best job you can. At the end of the day you're working for a company that is making products or providing a service for a profit, and hopefully the customer understands that. 'Business is Business.' Certain customers are angry and there is nothing you can do, within the company's policies, to make them happy. You can't give every angry customer a free year's supply of your product. And if the angry customer doesn't understand this then maybe he or she is not the kind of customer you want. However, always be polite—'I am offering you the best solution that I can. Which of these would you like to accept: the replacement item, the partial refund, or the store credit?' If the customer still doesn't accept, then say—'I apologize that the solution(s) I have offered are not acceptable to you; there is nothing more I can do for you today.'"

Question: "What do you do with an angry customer who doesn't stop talking? I couldn't get a word in edgewise."—*Transportation Authority*

Answer: "Yes, some customers love to talk and if it is just talking, your job is to politely move the conversation forward. Every customer has to catch their breath and that is the point where you must jump in with a redirecting question—'I think that is great, can you also let me have your address . . .' or 'Thank you for the information; I just need a few more details . . .'

"However, some people are so upset and so beside themselves that they've got to go through a two-minute rant. And in that case, just give them verbal noises like, oh, uh-huh and give them those encouraging sounds because once they have gotten rid of everything they need to say, they will become your most loyal customers. You have allowed them to vent. Most customers who are angry are angry about their life. Their anger has nothing to do with you and your company. You just happen to be the lucky one who receives it all. This call is the tipping point for them. Let them explode and then they become wonderful."

Question: "How can you deal with an angry customer without severing the ties?"
            —*Springfield Clinic*

Answer: "Again, you have to use truthfulness and honesty. 'I do want to retain you as a customer, and I apologize that everything we've done this far hasn't resolved the issue. Please allow me to come back to you next week when we can look at other options because, as I said, your business is important to me.' Or, 'I apologize because I understand this problem isn't being sorted out in this particular conversation. So I will work on it with my service department and I will get back to you by the end of the day.'"

▼

KEY POINT

Listen. Apologize. Tell the Truth.
Customers need to tell their side of the story before you jump in and give them solutions. They also hate to be lied to or feel that you don't care. So listen, apologize for the situation, and tell the truth.

Customers—Green, Yellow, Red

Customers fall into two main emotional categories: happy and unhappy. The happy customer is friendly and calm. The unhappy customer is frustrated and angry. If you were to think of customers in terms of traffic lights, here's how they would look:

Happy = Green = Go
Neutral = Yellow = Caution
Unhappy = Red = Stop

Creating Unhappy Customers

This chapter deals mainly with how to handle unhappy customers. However, it is important to know that happy customers can easily be triggered into becoming unhappy. For example, being put on hold too long or a misinterpreted tone of voice can trigger a change in their emotional state.

Let's explore how a happy customer turns into an unhappy one. The customer calls to check her account status. You may have just handled a very difficult customer and are still feeling the effects. You have tension in your voice. Suddenly the seemingly happy customer says:

> *"Do you talk to all your customers in that tone of voice? I might not be your biggest customer, but I've been using your company for 10 years now. I expect better treatment."*

Or you put the customer on hold to gather some information; you realize it's gone beyond the acceptable 30 seconds but you feel he will not mind. When you get him back on the phone, he says:

> *"I've been on hold for ages. I just called to check on my account, but you obviously don't care about my time. . . ."*

Or the customer expects to have the installation done the next day, and you have to tell her the earliest is two weeks!

> *"The salesperson said there would be no problem getting it installed. If I'd known it would take this long, I would have bought it from someone else! I may just cancel and do that!"*

One of the reasons that we take advantage of our *happy* customers is that we feel more at ease with them. It's much easier to use our skills with unhappy customers, because they are "squeakier wheels."

Super Service recommends that we "oil" both the *happy* and the *unhappy* customer. If we concentrate on using all of our communication skills with both types of customers, two things will happen:

1. The happy customer will remain happy.
2. The unhappy customer will become happy!

10 Keys to Handling an Unhappy Customer

When all fired up and angry, a customer doesn't have time to be friendly. So you have to assume the entire responsibility.

▼

KEY POINT

Your attitude is contagious. If you hold a friendly space for customers to vent their anger, they will calm down more quickly, and you will feel more in control and professional.

So fight fire with friendliness. On the next page are 10 keys to dealing with unhappy customers.

---

10 KEYS FOR DEFUSING UNHAPPY CUSTOMERS

1. Show empathy that you understand their situation.
   "I'm sorry."
2. Encourage venting to help them get rid of their anger.
   "Please tell me what happened."
3. Stay objective and don't take it personally.
   "I can understand how you would feel that way."
4. Remain calm to the situation by remaining peaceful.
   "I believe we can resolve this."
5. Listen attentively and show you are listening.
   "Aha, yes, I see."
6. Take responsibility and show urgency.
   "I will make sure this problem is resolved ASAP."
7. Involve the customer in the solution.
   "How would you like this handled?"
8. Give added value.
   "Another way we can help resolve this situation is . . ."
9. Provide an action plan.
   "This is what I propose to do . . ."
10. Involve your management.
    "I will make management aware of this problem."

Letting the Customer Vent

Let customers vent all their feelings, but do not take them on board. In other words, remain "nonemotional": This is not a personal attack. The customer is angry, and that's all there is to it. Here are some tips to use with a venting customer:

Never do these things with venting customers:

- Get angry yourself.
- Tell them to calm down.
- Defend yourself.
- Interrupt.
- Fail to acknowledge their anger.

Do these things with venting customers:

- Listen actively for what they want to happen.
- Allow their rage to burn itself out.
- Visualize them cooling down to green.
- Keep yourself calm by breathing calmly.
- Acknowledge their feelings.

It doesn't matter if customers are right or wrong, they need to air their complaint. If you do not treat them with care, you may lose them completely.

It's as if you are whitewater rafting. Your customer is the raging water, and you are taking great care to steer your raft to calmer waters. You don't allow yourself to get sucked in. The customer's words flow like water underneath you. Your breathing is calm, and on every exhalation, you let go of your own emotionality. Remember, the customer is simply angry! You could be the customer's mother/father/sibling/best friend/lover/teacher, and he or she would still be angry.

When customers are angry, there is nothing you can do except listen. Listening doesn't mean you agree with them; you are acting like a sounding board, and their words bounce off you without inflicting any pain.

One of the keys we mentioned is to accept responsibility. However, it's no good just saying it. You have to take action. On the following page is a tried-and-true recipe for accepting responsibility by taking action.

PLAN FOR TAKING ACTION

1. Write down what the customer says, to show that you are actively listening.
2. Use positive words:
    "Consider it done!"
3. Give your name:
    "My name is _____, and I will take care of this."
4. Show that their issue is your priority:
    "I will have an answer for you today."
5. Thank the customer for the opportunity:
    "Thank you for the opportunity to be of service."
6. Sound confident and responsive:
    "I am confident I can help."

Definitely avoid some phrases when dealing with unhappy customers. Here are some of them:

PHRASES TO AVOID

"I'll get to you in a minute."
"The company policy states . . ."
"I've been too busy to . . ."
"This never happens normally."
"I'm sorry, that's not my responsibility."

And here are some phrases to use:

PHRASES TO USE

"I will take care of you right away."

"How can I help?"

"It is my responsibility to help find a solution."

"Tell me more about this problem."

"That is quite a problem. I don't blame you for feeling upset."

"I'll make sure this gets corrected right away."

Sometimes when we communicate, we build barriers that stop the information from getting through. The barriers include everything from noise to judgments to prejudices. Here are some ways to overcome such barriers:

WAYS TO OVERCOME BARRIERS

1. Block out surrounding noise by focusing on your customer.
2. Gather knowledge about your company and customers so that you can provide informed solutions.
3. Mirror the customer's nonverbal cues.
4. Actively listen.
5. Don't allow your judgments or prejudices to interfere.
6. Be aware of your tone, posture, and attitude.

The Irate Customer

Sometimes unhappy customers can be savage. They can use foul language, scream, shout, rant, and rave. While it is important not to take their venting personally, taking abuse is part of your job. Here are some simple tactics to calm irate customers:

1. **Visualization.** See them as small, newborn babies screaming for attention and you are the only person around to feed them.
    Tip: Sit tight—they will stop eventually.
2. **Gentle reminder.** Bring them back to sanity by gently saying, "Is there something I have done to personally upset you? I would like to help you. Please give me a chance."
3. **Transfer.** Sometimes the customer is too wild for one person to handle. Say, "I think my manager may be able to help you."
4. **Call security.** If the customer seems likely to turn into a savage beast and become physical, call for security.

CHECK-IN

1. Think of a time when you were an unhappy customer.
    a. Can you remember how you felt?
    b. Did you suffer buyer's remorse?
    c. Were you concerned that the product or service did not meet your needs?
    d. Were you concerned that repairs to the product would cost more than its current value?
    e. Write down any other concerns you had.

        _____

2. How do you like to be handled when you are an unhappy customer?
    a. With a sense of urgency
    b. Reassured that the problem can be resolved
    c. That the person is confident and responsive
    d. That the repairs won't cost more than the product
    e. _____

Your task is to become aware of how you normally handle unhappy customers. This awareness will help you not only in your business life but in your personal life too.

ACTION

Think of either a happy customer you usually forget about or an unhappy customer you would like to have better customer relations with. What about building the relationship?

1. Choose an internal or external, happy or unhappy customer.
2. If applicable to your job, invite the person for lunch or coffee.
3. Call the customers to update them on new products or services.
4. Send a thank-you card for their business.
5. Think about how you can work together as a team.

Life is too short to hold grudges. Life is too hard to be in combative relationships. You can make the difference; you just need to make the choice.

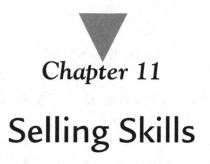

Chapter 11

Selling Skills

One of the key components of selling is to have great energy.

Here is how two of our clients, who participated in our *Super Service* workshop, answered the following three questions:

Barbara—Underwriters Laboratories Inc., Customer Service Team Project Lead

1. **As a customer, what do you want?**
   "To be encouraged that the problem will be solved by someone I can relate to."
2. **As a customer, what do you feel stops you from getting what you want?**
   "Bringing emotions, personal problems, and self-esteem issues into play."
3. **In your experience, what do customer service people do best?**
   "When they listen, handle the problem with no or hardly any hand-offs; being able to talk to a real person and reply within a reasonable timeline."

Kris—Underwriters Laboratories Inc., Customer Service Team Project Lead

1. **As a customer, what do you want?**
   "I want resolution."
2. **As a customer, what do you feel stops you from getting what you want?**
   "Customer service people who are not motivated to respond and complete a request in a timely or pleasant manner. Lack of communication. Someone who can make a decision."
3. **In your experience, what do customer service people do best?**
   "Good customer service people are those willing to go the extra mile for a client or a customer."

Up-Selling

In some customer service situations, you can add to your company's profits by up-selling. "Up-selling" is offering a suggestion to an already receptive buyer to enhance the value of his or her purchase.

You personally experience up-selling when you order an advertised product and the order taker automatically offers you an additional related product at a special discount. For example, every buyer experiences up-selling when Amazon.com offers an additional related book for a slight discount.

Just to clarify between up-selling and cross-selling: cross-selling is almost the same as up-selling. "Cross-selling" offers a similar product to what a customer is looking for. For example, when Amazon.com automatically lists other books purchased by people who bought the same book you just ordered, that is cross-selling.

With up-selling, you are using *new* skills to help make your job as interesting as you choose it to be. Professional customer service providers or reps are a resource for their customers; being the value-added professional creates job satisfaction. By helping your customer decide to buy a little extra or upgrade slightly what he or she already has, you are making the customer feel truly taken care of. Remember, if you don't try . . . it is 100 percent NO; if you try, you are getting a 50 percent chance of a YES!

Stop thinking that you are bothering people when you are up-selling to them. Begin seeing up-selling as a "service" that you are giving your customers. Surveys show that most buyers appreciate being told about additional products or services that might better meet their needs, or new items that were not offered in the past.

▼

KEY POINT

Up-selling provides your customers with an additional service. You are giving them information about products and services which will enhance what they are already purchasing.

Up-selling is a way of demonstrating that you are aware of your customers' needs and care about their satisfaction. The bottom line or the key to successful up-selling is to focus efforts on meeting your customers' needs, rather than simply pushing more products and services on them, so that everyone benefits.

When you have taken care of their needs, fixed their problems, recapped, and made them feel that you have "taken care" of them, now is the ideal time to say something like:

"Mr. Jones, in reviewing your account, I see that you have a compressor. There are a lot of popular accessories that go with that, such as compressor oil, ball valves, hose, and more. Would you like to hear more about them?" (Ask permission to proceed.)

Up-selling should be a natural part of the conversation. If you are selling a pump, for example, you can also offer a hose and couplers to hook them together. To gain the extra sale, you might simply have to mention that the other products are available.

Here are some do's and don'ts in up-selling:

DO'S

- Do fully complete the original sale *before* up-selling.
- Do offer familiar items.
- Do provide useful advice based on other customer purchases.

"Many of our customers who order a _____ also order a _____ to go with it. Would you like one also?"

Do think of up-selling as a dessert. Picture yourself in a nice restaurant after a lovely meal. The waiter comes by to see if you would like dessert. Perhaps you are too full from dinner to consider it, but you are certainly not offended by being asked. "Other customers have been really enjoying our excellent desserts tonight—I'd be happy to show you . . ."

DON'TS

- Don't rush to offer the add-on product. It may turn the customer off.
- Don't up-sell new products. They take too long to explain,
- Don't over-sell. Customers have a mental limit of what they will spend.
- Don't force the up-sell on every customer. It may damage the service component.

▼

KEY POINT

Up-selling works the best when it is a natural part of the conversation and not a hard sell. Up-selling is just an opportunity to tell customers about their options.

Here is a sample conversation of a customer service rep (CSR) up-selling to a customer:

CSR: "Thank you for calling Greenco, this is Sarah, how may I help you?"

Customer: "This is Fred from Jones Electrical Contracting. I need to pick up a dozen flashlights this afternoon."

CSR: "Excellent, Fred. What kind of flashlight do you need?"

Customer: "I have a number here: 2V930."

CSR: "Great! That's a Mag-Lite flashlight."

Circle the correct up-sell question:

Question A: "Each of them takes three D-size batteries. Would you like batteries on this order as well?"

Question B: "What else would you like today?"

Question C: "You have 12 Mag-Lite flashlights. We'll have that waiting for you at our will-call counter. Okay?"

CSR: "Each of them takes three D-size batteries. Would you like batteries on this order as well? (*Question A is correct.*)

Customer: "Yes, that would be good."

Circle the correct up-sell question:

Question A: "Our D-size batteries come in packs of 12. Would you like three packs?"

Question B: "What else would you like today?"

Question C: "Our D-size batteries come in packs of 12. Would you like three packs, or would you like a spare pack as well?"

CSR: "Our D-size batteries come in packs of 12. Would you like three packs or would you like a spare pack as well?" (*Question C is correct.*)

Customer: "Why don't you give me four packs of 12."

CSR: "Perfect Fred. Would you like belt holsters to go with those?"

Customer: "No thanks. I have all that stuff."

CSR: "Okay, so you have 12 Mag-Lite flashlights and four packs of D-size batteries. Your total is $192.30. We'll have that waiting at our will-call counter."

Customer: "Sounds great."

CSR: "Thank you, Fred for calling Greenco. We appreciate your business. Have a wonderful day!"

▼

KEY POINT

Write down a list of your top-selling products. Next to them, write down additional products that you could up-sell to your customers. Keep the list where you can see it.

Super Service providers are also salespeople. You are always selling yourself, your services, or your company. If you think about it, the whole world is a gigantic sales machine. Selling is not just confined to sales and marketing; selling involves every walk of life, including politics, healthcare, school districts, construction, space projects, and so on.

As a *Super Service* provider, you can offer your customers better service when you understand the six sales situations that you may provide them with a solution:

1. The service or product does not fit the customer's needs.
2. An additional part/process/program/piece is needed to make the product/ service function properly.
3. The product or service is out-of-date.
4. A new upgrade will enhance the product or service.
5. The customer has outgrown the product or service.
6. A competitive system or product is incompatible with yours.

Not all service situations can be answered by a sale. In some situations, selling is a definite no-no! Here are four examples:

1. Your product or service does not and will never meet the customer's needs.
2. The product or service created a big problem for the customer and he or she wants to stay mad.
3. An upgrade provides no additional benefit.
4. The product or service is defective and needs to be exchanged.

What *can* you do in such situations?

The OPEN Technique

"Selling" is the ability to get the commitment from people to say "yes" to products or services. As a *Super Service* provider you have the opportunity to up-sell, and we want to give you the very best technique. The sales technique is called OPEN, an acronym for a series of questions—**O**pening, **P**robing, **E**ffect, **N**ail down—that enable the *Super Service* provider to identify the customer's needs. The technique can be easily learned and used in any situation. Here is the basic formula:

O   **Opening questions.** Start the sale by understanding the background.
P   **Probing questions.** Reveal problems, difficulty, or dissatisfaction.
E   **Effect questions.** Explode the problems into other areas.
N   **Nail down questions.** Develop solutions that address needs.

Opening Questions

Let's say your product does not fit the customer's needs. Your first job is to gather background information. It doesn't matter if you are in the clothing business (*"What kind of function are you attending?"*) or scrap metal (*"How do you organize your scrap recovery?"*). An "opening question" gives you background information that will help you uncover the customer's need.

Safe

It is safe to ask "opening questions" with new customers, either early in the conversation or when the customer's situation has changed.

Hazardous

It is hazardous to ask "opening questions" late in the conversation, in sensitive areas, or when you sound like an interrogator by asking too many questions.

Probing Questions

Once you understand the background, you need to know the specific problem. If you work for a car-manufacturing company, the question could be: *"What kind of quality issues do you experience?"* For a food wholesaler, the question could be: *"Is there any part of your operation that is costing you too much money?"* A "probing question" begins to examine areas where your customer is experiencing problems.

Safe

It is safe to ask "probing questions" early in the conversation, in areas where your product or service can provide solutions, or in areas that are significant to your customer.

Hazardous

It is hazardous to ask "probing questions" in sensitive areas such as where organizational politics run high, where the customer has a high personal or emotional involvement, or where your product or service does not provide a solution.

Effect Questions

If you know the problem, you can explode it into other areas to create an even greater need: *"What effect does this situation have on your delivery system?" "How do the breakdowns impact employee morale?"* An "effect question" helps customers realize that the problem reaches into other areas. It gives customers additional reasons for seeking a solution.

Safe

It is safe to ask "effect questions" when problems are significant and complex.

Hazardous

It is hazardous to ask "effect questions" too early in the conversation or in situations that you cannot solve.

Nail Down Questions

Customers buy because they have needs. "Nail down questions" help the customer realize the gain of your solution. Again, it doesn't matter if you work for a catering service (*"If you save 10 cents a plate, how much would that mean in total savings?"*) or for a swimming pool manufacturer (*"How much would the self-clean process reduce your maintenance costs?"*).

Safe

It is safe to ask "nail down questions" when they pay off in other areas or when the solutions must be justified by the customer.

Hazardous

It is hazardous to ask "nail down questions" too early in the conversation.

Energy

One of the key components of selling is to have great energy. Let's look at a couple of case studies in energy.

Energy for Selling: Barbara the Receptionist

A construction company we consult with has the best receptionist we've ever met. She sells her company just by her upbeat energy. Her name is Barbara and we asked how she does it:

> "One of my main motivations for responding to callers in an enthusiastic and gracious manner is quite simply because that's the way I like to be treated. There is nothing more unappealing than to call a business office and have the person answer the phone sounding as if they are doing you a favor by answering your call.

> "Another motivation is selfishness. When I act in a positive, cheerful manner, people usually respond to me accordingly. Others often start to mirror my enthusiastic demeanor. All of us have days when we feel lethargic and less lively than others. But if you act as though you were energetic and positive, you start to feel that way. You start to fool people into believing you feel great! That's what I try to do.

> "People often perceive the receptionist to be merely the person who picks up a ringing telephone. The job is considered by many to be uncreative and routine. On the contrary, I think of it as the first opportunity to make a good and memorable impression on a customer or a potential customer. By interacting positively with all types of personalities, from all walks of life, the receptionist is constantly creating a rapport and a relationship for his or her company."

Here are the main points for having great energy:

1. Be enthusiastic and gracious.
2. Act in a positive and cheerful manner.
3. In a frontline job, make the first impression good and memorable.
4. Create a good rapport and relationship with the customer.

Energy for Selling: Carol, the Salesperson

In comparison to Barbara the Receptionist, our salesperson, Carol, focuses on being assertive and persistent—persistent in a professional sense. It doesn't mean being rude or obnoxious and calling all the time. Carol believes that she has something worthwhile to say and do, and her energy conveys that message to her customers. Here is what Carol says about her job:

> "My motto is, I might not be seeing you this month, but I will be seeing you! If a company has a need for our service, it becomes like a game. 'All I want is 20 minutes of your time. I believe we have an outstanding service; if you give me that 20 minutes, I'll show you how we can help you to increase sales, have happier, more motivated employees, and satisfy 100 percent of your customers, 100 percent of the time!'"

If Carol took rejection personally, she would not be able to do her job. Often, she gets rejected, treated without respect, and told to call back next month or next year.

1. **Persistence:** "I'm here to make an appointment with you, and it's going to happen sooner or later."
2. **Focus:** "I know what I want from this call, and I will keep directing it back to my goal."
3. **Assertive:** "I know how much our services have helped other companies like yours; we just want the opportunity to discuss your needs."
4. **Energy:** "I don't take rejection personally. I move on to the next call."

Here is how Carol's persistence worked with U.S. Robotics before they became 3Com. She had driven past their company and wanted to do business with them. She got the name of the person she needed to talk with and called. She called every day and got either the person's assistant or voice mail. Carol would come into the office and before she even took off her coat, she dialed the number, and she would dial it at different times throughout the day. One day we said to her, "Don't tell us you're still trying to get in there!" We all laughed.

Finally, Carol was told the person had left the company. That still didn't stop her. Carol kept calling until she was given another name. Five calls later she got through to another person and was immediately given an appointment. It took 347 calls over a 10-month period. Now that U.S. Robotics/3Com, has seen the kind of work we and our salespeople do, they have become one of our major customers.

As Carol says, "One of two things has to happen: They either give me the appointment, or they have to tell me to stop calling!"

CHECK-IN

Next time you are selling, consider this list of skills:

1. Be able to maintain an enthusiastic and positive attitude.
2. Want to do the best for the customer.
3. Know the basic selling skills.
4. Want the customer to be left with a great lasting impression.
5. Be aware of both the internal and external customers.

To be a great salesperson you need to have:

1. Persistence, assertiveness, focus, energy.
2. Objectivity—Do not take rejection personally.
3. Belief in your product or service.

Chapter 12

Telephone Skills

In the business world, the telephone is like a screwdriver:
It can open things, close things, and it can also screw things up.

Here is how one of our clients, who participated in our *Super Service* workshop, answered the following three questions:

Lisa—*Healthcare Ultrasound & Primary Care Diagnostics, Demo Asset Manager*

1. **As a customer, what do you want?**

   "*A predictable, positive experience.*"

2. **As a customer, what do you feel stops you from getting what you want?**

   "*Variation in people and process. (I put people first because they can choose whether to follow the process—good or bad.)*"

3. **In your experience, what do customer service people do best?**

   "*Make you feel like you are their sole focus at the time. Making YOU happy is their mission.*"

Every time your telephone rings, think of it as your paycheck calling. Because your telephone is a customer touch point—it reinforces your company brand—used effectively, it can provide the repetition necessary to inspire your customers to continue to buy from you.

There is also something called "on-brand" and "off-brand." For example, if you say in your advertising literature that *the customer is number one*, but, when the customer calls he or she can never get someone to answer the telephone, then your standards for answering the telephone are "off-brand."

When you think about the telephone as tied into your paycheck, as a sales-building tool, you will be more likely to answer the telephone with a positive and upbeat tone rather than a bored, or indifferent tone. Interesting statistics show that people develop a perception about you within the first 30 seconds of a telephone conversation and their final opinion of you in the last 30 seconds. So here are some telephone tips that will help boost that final opinion so that customers leave the telephone call feeling like they are happy to be your customers—or in marketing terms—building an ongoing, on brand, positive relationship!

1. **Breathe!** Before you pick up the telephone, take a deep breath. Most of us are "shallow breathers." We take small breaths in and out, and as a result we sound tired when we answer the telephone. Your goal on every telephone call is to sound as if you are glad the customer called and you enjoy your job.

▼

KEY POINT

Try this: Take a big breath and answer the telephone at the top of that breath. Continue speaking on the exhale and the caller will hear the energy in your voice! You can also practice it when you are making a telephone call. Start your breath as the telephone is ringing on the other end. You'll be surprised how you feel when you use this technique.

2. **Identify yourself**. State your name and the company name. Here is an example: "Thank you for calling Greenco. This is Mary Spence. How can I make it a great day for you?" This may sound hokey, but it is definitely friendly and you can have fun with it.

3. **Slow down.** When you answer the telephone or when you call to leave a message, make sure you slow down so that the person on the other end has a chance to hear what you are saying. If you have ever had to replay your answering machine or messages to understand what the person is saying, you will know this is true.

4. **Customers are first.** Put your customer's needs ahead of your own. I was recently told of a customer who had picked out the merchandise but when she got to the counter to pay for it, the customer service provider took a telephone call from a friend and just ignored the customer. Finally the customer walked out and left the store without buying anything.

5. **Listen attentively.** When you answer the telephone, put everything down. Don't answer your e-mail, sip a cup of coffee, or go through your folders. No one is really good at multitasking. If you are not focused on your customer's wants and needs, you are throwing away an opportunity to be great.

6. **Take notes.** Take notes on what your customer is saying. Use a headset if possible, to keep your hands free. By taking notes you can verify with your customer, as well as with yourself, the important points of the conversation and the action items that need attention.

7. **Visualize the customer.** Even if you don't know your customer, you can visualize how you think he or she looks. This way, you remind yourself that you are engaged in a two-way conversation with a human being. This will help you listen attentively and find solutions.

8. **Outcome.** The first 30 seconds will establish a positive perception about you through your voice, tone, and focus. The last 30 seconds will be when the caller finalizes his or her opinion about you. You can make that a positive experience by thanking the customer for calling, reviewing the problem you were able to solve, and most importantly, thanking the customer for his or her continued business.

Customers Always Have a Choice

Because I fly all over the world, I have a great deal of experience with airlines and I notice that every pilot has "air time" with the passengers. The words that pilots use are much the same, no matter what airline. They talk about the weather in the city we are headed to, arrival time, not to congregate in the aisles, where the lavatories are located, and how great the flight attendants are. Then, they always say:

> *"We know you have a choice of airlines when you travel. We are happy that you have chosen to fly with us. We ask that if your future travel plans involve flying, you will think of us first. So sit back, relax, and enjoy the on-time flight to. . . ."*

A great outcome is being set up by the pilot. Even though he cannot see his passengers, he starts by building a trusting relationship with them by coming across as very approachable. Then he gives information about the most important things we should know about the flight and who will help us if we have a problem. Finally, he asks for our repeat business. The trust is built on the sound and sincerity of the pilot's voice.

It's just the same when you talk to your customers. To build a strong business, you need to have repeat and referral business. What easier way to get repeat business than to ask for their continued business at the end of each and every telephone call: "Thank you for calling. I ask that next time you think of purchasing a . . . , you think of us first. Enjoy your . . ."

KEY POINT

The way you speak over the telephone conveys 85 percent of your message, so focus on making it a smooth flight each and every time your telephone rings.

Telephone Tips

People will make assumptions about you, just by your telephone skills. So here are a couple of tips right off the bat:

1. Return calls immediately.
2. Keep messages short, and include the response you need.

One manager we know fast-forwards to the end of long-winded messages; any vital information in the middle is lost. If you are guilty of leaving endless telephone messages, here is what to do:

Call yourself and leave a lengthy message.
Play it back, jot down three key points, and turn the points into *one* short sentence.
Call yourself again and leave the shortened message.
Play it back and notice the difference.

Here is another exercise. Read this message and highlight the key point:

My name is Brown, my number is 900-3000, and I need an estimate for a Model 60 unit. I need to update it because I've had the older version, which I got from your competitor, for over three years. It's time for a new one! I heard about your company from a friend of mine, and they were very happy with your product and service. It seems that the new plastic coating works well in my type of environment. I work in a—well, I can tell you about that when you return my call (ha, ha). I'm in the building from 8:00 A.M. to 5:00 P.M. (I try to get out by 4:00 P.M., but not today—worst luck.) My lunch hour is twelve 'til one. If I'm not here when you call, please leave a message, and I will get right back to you. Oh, I'd also like to know about any volume discounts. There are some other people who may be interested. People in finance and H.R., but we can talk about that when you call. Look forward to hearing from you. Again my number is 900-3000 and my name is Brown! Thanks, and have a great day!"

Get to the point! NAME, NUMBER, AND THE REASON FOR THE CALL. The first sentence said it all.

The Effect of Your Voice

Your voice sounds different from the voice of other people. Your voice is unique to you and reflects your personality and inner attitude. If you are angry, you will sound angry. Voices can be annoying or pleasant to listen to. They can be clear, squeaky, difficult to decipher, monotonous, low-pitched, or high-pitched.

Four factors determine how your voice sounds:

- Rate of speech
- Volume
- Tone
- Diction

The energy you put into your voice reflects your attitude, enthusiasm, and willingness to serve. If you are soft-spoken, it can seem as though you don't know what you are talking about. If you are loud, you can seem overbearing. Adjust the volume of your voice to your customer's volume unless, of course, the customer is shouting and angry!

Choose words that can be easily understood. Be caring and confident. Speak at a rate that is neither too fast nor too slow. The following passage is 140 words in length. Using the second hand of your watch, time yourself while you read it aloud:

There is no set rule for the rate of speaking of individuals. Some persons can speak at a rate of one hundred ninety words per minute and be clearly understood, while others must speak as slowly as ninety words per minute to achieve the same understanding. Most experts feel, however, that there is more to be gained by **speaking slowly.** *They have decided that a rate of about one hundred forty words per minute is a safe rate. The main disadvantage of speaking too fast is that you* *cannot be understood easily. Speaking too fast has other disadvantages. Your client may get the impression of being high-pressured into something. In addition, your client may get the impression that you are very rushed and concerned with time. To be really understood, we recommend that you speak slowly.* **One hundred forty! One forty!**

The Faceless Voice on the Line

Here is another telephone phenomenon: You have no idea (unless you are on a video-conference call) what the other people are doing, who they are with, or where they are. With call forwarding, they could be on another continent.

We know a person who took his business to Florida and never told any customers. If there was a problem, he would fly in, take care of it, and fly out again. Never make assumptions with the telephone.

You could be talking about someone who is standing right next to the person you are calling. Have you ever done this? A person with a loud voice calls, you have to hold the telephone away from your ear, and everyone in the room hears!

Don't be paranoid about the telephone, but do treat it with respect. In the business world the telephone is like a screwdriver: It can open things, close things, and screw things up.

Your Effectiveness on the Telephone

Ask yourself this:

"Do I help my customers?"
"Do I use empathy and understanding?"
"Do I sleep at night knowing that I've done the best job I could do?"

Here are some *Super Service* affirmations to help you prepare.

SUPER SERVICE AFFIRMATIONS

1. *My customer is anyone who isn't me!*
2. I keep an open mind.
3. I allow people to speak.
4. I repeat their message for clear understanding.
5. I keep my tone light.
6. I sit up straight.
7. I concentrate on the conversation.
8. I smile when I dial.
9. I vary my pace.
10. I stay interested.
11. I answer by the second or third ring.
12. I provide my company name and department.
13. I give my name.
14. I ask, "How may I help you?"
15. I am courteous.
16. I am willing.
17. I am giving.
18. I take responsibility.
19. I am friendly.
20. I enjoy the telephone.

HOW TO TRANSFER A CALL

T   **Take** time to communicate:
"Linda in accounts will be able to answer your question."

R   **Request** permission:
"May I add Linda to our call?"

A   **Add** calls while remaining on the line:
"I'll stay on the line until Linda joins our call."

N   **Never** use the term "transfer":
"Linda will be added to our call. Is that all right?"

S   **Stay** on the line until the problem is resolved:
"Thank you for holding. This is Linda from accounts, Mr. Bachman; I've explained your problem to her. Linda, this is Mr. Bachman."

F   **Focus** on solving all the customer's issues:
"Is there anything else that I can help you with today?"

E   **Empathize** with your customers:
"I know how frustrating this must have been for you. I hope the problem has been resolved to your satisfaction."

R   **Remember** you can make this a great experience:
"I'm very pleased to be of service. Is there anything else I can help you with?"

HOW TO TAKE AN ACCURATE MESSAGE

- Record the time and date on a message pad.
- Ask for the company name, the caller's name, and the telephone number.
- Ask for and write the message clearly.
- Repeat all of the above for accuracy.
- Ask for the best time to return the telephone call.
- State, "I will give her the message."
- Sign the message.
- Place the message where it can be clearly seen (or leave it in voice mail or e-mail, if the person is not available).

Using the Telephone with a Computer

We consulted with a customer service department for a large marine company. The customer service providers sit with telephone terminals in their ears, looking at their computer screens. They deal with agents who purchase their equipment.

The customer service provider needs the agent's number to access all of the agent's on-screen information. The customer service provider is so focused on getting the agent's number that the first words out of his or her mouth is, "What's your number?" Even angry customers are greeted with, "What's your number?"

Has that ever happened to you? It is like being discounted. A better way to answer calls is to listen to at least one or two sentences of the customer's problem. Then, when you have some understanding of the issues, say:

> *"I understand your problem. May I have your agent number so I can help you by seeing all of your information on my screen?"*

Some management has the philosophy that if they get the call rate as high as possible, they are providing good customer service. In reality, all that is happening is that their figures look good—thankfully, this is not happening across the board; in fact some companies are going above and beyond to create amazing *Super Service* within their company.

Red Line for Internal Use

I love to hear stories from our clients about what they have done to incorporate *Super Service*. One of our clients launched a Red Line as a resource for their employees. Designed specifically for internal use, it is a dedicated one-stop helpline covering products and services, IT and HR issues. It gives access to information, so people can get answers to their own questions as well as being more efficient in responding to their customers' needs.

On Red Line, they answer questions about anything to do with the company's products and services; the offer also extends to friends and families.

About 100 queries come in every day, 60 percent of them made on behalf of family members. The Red Line teams have to keep up to date with all the latest information. They need to know about all of our products, offers, and services. So they use the intranet site and consult on a daily basis with almost every department across the company to track down information. In that sense, they're constantly training themselves, and if they don't know the answer it's their job to know who to ask.

Their rate of efficiency is outstanding. They are able to answer 90 percent of questions immediately; but it's the other 10 percent that makes their job really interesting. Recently someone called as a last resort. He'd sent a phone in for repair some two years earlier, but the phone had been misplaced and had never been found. He'd tried customer services, the repair center, and other colleagues but with no luck. Finally he asked the Red Line if they could help. Within one week they'd tracked it down. However, because the phone was two years out of date they arranged for a replacement to be sent . . . now that's what we call *Super Service*!

Chapter 13

How to Avoid Stress and Burnout

You can foresee stress.
You can foresee burnout.
You can plan how to handle them.

Here is how one of our clients, who participated in our *Super Service* workshop, answered the following three questions:

Christopher—GE Healthcare Financial Services, Manager

1. **As a customer, what do you want?**

   "I want someone to empathize with my situation (or at least pretend to) and solve the issue. The worst thing is if I get bounced around from person to person and stuck in phone jail. I want to feel like I am their most important customer at that point in time."

2. **As a customer, what do you feel stops you from getting what you want?**

   "I feel that a straight adherence to policy and not commonsense, gets in the way of me getting what I want. Now I am not advocating people throw the rules out and do what they want, but in most cases, just using your head can make all the difference in the world to a customer. An example is if a customer calls for one thing, then realizes they need something else . . . help them. Don't just drop the call to the other team because that is what the SOP says."

3. **In your experience, what do customer service people do best?**

   "Customer service people take a lot of grief from many people communicating from their animal brain. The best customer service people rise above that and do not exchange comment for comment. They exceed the customer's expectations and go out of their way to make the customer feel satisfied. Everyone wants to feel special, and if you treat the customer like he or she is special you can help the customer, and probably save that relationship long-term. In my competitive environment, price reduction only gets you so far. Customers care less about price and more about service than people realize."

Stress and Relaxation

When you get stressed out, or feel angry, upset, anxious, tense, frustrated, or worried, adrenaline goes into your bloodstream. Adrenaline is good if you need to escape from a lion or a tiger, because it makes your heart beat faster and gives you energy to run. But in normal circumstances, adrenaline just puts strain on your cardiovascular system. This strain builds up so that later in life, things can go wrong because of it.

Every time you are able to lessen the intensity of stress, anger, tension, or worry, it will benefit your health. It also makes life a more pleasant experience.

Relaxation is the key. Relaxation is the antidote for stress. When you relax, you automatically lower your stress level, and therefore your adrenaline level and the strain on your cardiovascular system. But sometimes it is difficult to relax, especially when you are feeling worried.

These simple methods—breathing deeply, relaxing tense muscles, and saying the word "relax" to yourself—are easy to do. They can be done in the middle of your work, between telephone calls, after a particularly difficult telephone call, or before a meeting. These methods will slow your heart rate down to a healthier level. When you become more relaxed, you think better, you are more creative, and you can communicate more effectively. You will get along with your customers and coworkers in a more pleasant way, and your life will be smooth and agreeable. Using these relaxing methods will become a habit that you can use any time you feel stressed.

Breathing Deeply

Here is a very simple way to relax—it's called "breathing deeply." When you tense up, your breathing gets quicker, more shallow, and higher in the chest. The way to offset this is to breathe deeply. Take a deep breath and you will immediately feel better. Your heart rate will slow down and the strain on your cardiovascular system will lessen.

▼

Key Point

To breathe deeply, breathe in three times like this: Take a deep breath in and fill up your lungs. Then before you breathe out, breathe in a little more. Then before you breathe out, fill up your lungs as much as possible. Hold the breath to the count of three, and slowly breathe out. Repeat this a couple of times and you will feel your stress being exhaled from your mind and body.

Loosen Tensed Muscles

When you have adrenaline pumping, your muscles tighten, particularly the muscles around your neck, upper back, and face. Pay attention to your muscles in those areas. When you find a muscle contracting for no good reason, relax it. If at first you have trouble relaxing a muscle, tense it first, and then relax it.

▼

KEY POINT

To relax a tense muscle, first tense up the muscle as much as you can. Let's practice with your neck muscle. Tense your neck, tense it as much as possible, and then let go. Did you notice that when you tensed the muscle, you stopped breathing? After you have tensed a muscle and let go, breathe deeply and feel all of the stress exhale from the muscle.

Say "Relax"

Say the word "relax" to yourself. Make sure your inner voice is relaxing. Don't yell at yourself, "Relax!!" Say it soothingly: Relax, relax, relax.

▼

KEY POINT

Relax by saying the word "relax" to yourself in a soothing, relaxed voice. Feel your shoulders let go of the tension. Feel your back and neck muscles let go of the tension. Feel the word "relax," move around your body until you feel yourself completely and totally relaxed.

Additional Relaxation Exercises

Over the next few pages are some more methods for relieving stress. This next exercise is about "focusing":

EXERCISE 1—FOCUSING

Think of a flower. Focus all of your attention on the flower as you inhale and exhale slowly and deeply for one to two minutes. If any other thoughts come into your head while you are doing this exercise, just let them pass through your mind without paying them any particular attention. Return your attention to the flower. At the end of this exercise you will feel peaceful and calm.

EXERCISE 2—MEDITATION

Sit in a comfortable position—you can also lie down if you are at home. Close your eyes and breathe deeply. Let your breathing be slow and relaxed. Focus all of your attention on your breathing. Notice the movement of your chest and abdomen, in and out. Block out all other thoughts, feelings, and sensations. If you feel your attention wandering, bring it back to your breathing. As you inhale, say the word "peace" to yourself, and as you exhale, say the word "calm." Draw out the pronunciation of the word so that it lasts for the entire breath. The word "peace" sounds like p-e-e-a-a-c-c-c-e-e. The word "calm" sounds like: c-a-a-a-l-l-l-l-m-m-m. Repeat these words as you breathe and continue this exercise until you feel very relaxed.

EXERCISE 3—OAK TREE MEDITATION

Sit in a comfortable position, your arms resting at your sides. Close your eyes and breathe deeply. Let your breathing be slow and relaxed. Visualize your body as a strong oak tree. Your body is solid like the wide, brown trunk of the tree. Imagine sturdy roots growing from your legs and going down deeply into the earth, anchoring your body. You feel solid and strong, able to handle any stress. When upsetting thoughts or situations occur, visualize your body remaining grounded like the oak tree. Feel the strength and stability in your arms and legs. By the end of this exercise, you will feel confident, relaxed, and able to handle any situation.

EXERCISE 4—RELEASING TENSION THROUGH THE COLOR BLUE

In many studies, scientists have exposed subjects to specific colors, either directly through exposure to light therapy, or through changing the color of their environment. Scientific research throughout the world has shown that color therapy can have a profound effect on health and well-being. It can stimulate the endocrine glands, the immune system, and the nervous system, and help to balance the emotions. Visualizing color in a specific part of the body can have a powerful therapeutic effect, too, and can be a good stress management technique for relief of anxiety and nervous tension.

This exercise uses the color blue, which provides a calming and relaxing effect. For people with anxiety who carry a lot of physical and emotional tension, blue lessens the fight-or-flight response. Blue also calms such physiological functions as pulse rate, breathing, and perspiration, and relaxes the mood. If you experience chronic fatigue and are tense, anxious, or irritable, or carry a lot of muscle tension, this exercise will be very helpful.

Sit in a comfortable position, your arms resting at your sides. As you take a deep breath, visualize that the earth below you is filled with the color blue. This blue color extends 50 feet below you into the earth. Now imagine that you are opening up energy centers on the bottom of your feet. As you inhale, visualize the soft blue color filling up your feet. When your feet are completely filled with the color blue, bring the color up through your ankles, legs, pelvis, and lower back.

Each time you exhale, see the blue color leaving through your lungs, carrying any tension and stress with it. See the tension dissolve into the air.

Continue to inhale the blue color into your abdomen, chest, shoulders, arms, neck, and head. Exhale the blue color slowly out of your lungs. Repeat this entire process five times and then relax for a few minutes.

EXERCISE 5—RELEASING TENSION THROUGH THE COLOR RED

This exercise uses the color red, which can benefit people who have fatigue due to chronic anxiety and upset. Red stimulates all of the endocrine glands, including the pituitary and adrenal glands. It heightens senses such as smell and taste. Emotionally, red is linked to vitality and high energy states. Even though the color red can speed up the autonomic nervous system function, people with anxiety-related fatigue can benefit from visualizing this color. You may find that you are attracted to the color in one exercise more than another. Use the exercise with the color that appeals to you the most.

Sit or lie in a comfortable position, your arms resting easily at your sides. As you take a deep breath, visualize a big balloon above your head filled with a bright red healing energy. Imagine that you pop this balloon so all the bright red energy is released. As you inhale, see the bright red color filling up your head. It fills up your brain, your face, and the bones of your skull. Let the bright red color pour in until your head is ready to overflow with color. Then let the red color flow into your neck, shoulders, arms, and chest. As you exhale, breathe the red color out of your lungs, taking any tiredness and fatigue with it. Breathe any feeling of fatigue out of your body.

As you inhale, continue to bring the bright, energizing red color into your abdomen, pelvis, lower back, legs, and feet until your whole body is filled with red. Exhale the red color out of your lungs, continuing to release any feeling of fatigue. Repeat this process five times. At the end of this exercise, you should feel energized and vibrant. Your mental energy should feel vitalized and clear.

EXERCISE 6—POSITIVE AFFIRMATIONS TO RELIEVE ANXIETY

This exercise will give you healthful affirmations that are very useful for people with anxiety. Stress and anxiety symptoms are due to a complex interplay between the mind and body. Your state of emotional and physical health is determined in part by the thousands of mental messages you send yourself each day with your thoughts. For example, if a fear of public places triggers your anxiety symptoms, the mind will send a constant stream of messages to you reinforcing your beliefs about the dangers and mishaps that can occur in public places. The fright triggers muscle tension and shallow breathing. Similarly, if you constantly criticize the way you look, your lack of self-love may be reflected in your body. For example, your shoulders may slump and you may have a dull and lackluster countenance.

Affirmations provide a method to change these negative belief systems to thoughts that preserve peace and calm. Positive statements replace the anxiety-inducing messages with thoughts that make you feel good.

This affirmation exercise gives you a series of statements to promote a sense of emotional and physical health and well-being. Using these affirmations will create a feeling of emotional peace by changing your negative beliefs about your body and health into positive beliefs. Repeat these phrases as often as you want.

- I handle stress and tension appropriately and effectively.
- My mood is calm and relaxed.
- I can cope well and get on with my life during times of stress.
- I think thoughts that uplift and nurture me.
- I enjoy thinking positive thoughts that make me feel good about myself and my life.
- I deserve to feel good right now.
- I feel peaceful and calm.
- My breathing is slow and calm.
- My muscles are relaxed and comfortable.
- I feel grounded and fully present.
- I can effectively handle any situation that comes my way.
- I think through the solutions to my emotional issues slowly and peacefully.
- I am thankful for all the positive things in my life.
- I practice the relaxation methods that I enjoy.

- My body is healthy and strong.
- I eat a well-balanced and nutritious diet.
- I enjoy eating delicious and healthful food.
- My body wants food that is easy to digest and high in vitamins and minerals.
- I do regular exercise in a relaxed and enjoyable manner.

EXERCISE 7—POSITIVE AFFIRMATIONS TO IMPROVE SELF-ESTEEM AND SELF-CONFIDENCE

This affirmation exercise helps promote self-esteem and self-confidence and also helps to reduce anxiety. Many people with high anxiety lose their self-confidence and feel depressed and defeated by their condition. They feel frustrated and somehow at fault for not finding a solution. Repeat each affirmation to yourself or say them out loud for 3 to 5 minutes. Use either this or the previous exercise on a regular basis to promote healthful, positive thought patterns.

- I am filled with energy, vitality, and self-confidence.
- I am pleased with how I handle my emotional needs.
- I know exactly how to manage my daily schedule to promote my emotional and physical well-being.
- I listen to my body's needs and regulate my activity level to take care of those needs.
- I love and honor my body.
- I fill my mind with positive and self-nourishing thoughts.
- I am a wonderful and worthy person.
- I deserve health, vitality, and peace of mind.
- I have total confidence in my ability to heal myself.
- I feel radiant with abundant energy and vitality.
- The world around me is full of radiant beauty and abundance.
- I am attracted only to those people and situations that support and nurture me.
- I appreciate the positive people and situations that are currently in my life.
- I love and honor myself.
- I enjoy my positive thoughts and feelings.

Allow Customers to Vent

Imagine a high-wire performer. Halfway through the act, the wire gets so stressed it snaps and the performer falls.

Imagine a forest. A blazing fire spreads out of control and burns every tree (including mature redwoods and young saplings).

The high-wire performer wasn't stressed, and the forest didn't start the fire; however, both suffered as a result of coming into contact with stress and burnout.

Fortunately, you are neither a high-wire performer nor a tree. You don't have to stand completely still or take terrifying risks. You are a *Super Service* provider—a professional whose job is to deal with customers.

Customers are your potential wires and fires. Even though they are not part of you, they can affect you so that you feel stressed and burned out. This happens when you ignore the signals.

A wise person once said, "God always sends pebbles before the rocks." So the best way to avoid stress and burnout is to take notice of the pebbles.

▼

KEY POINT

If you know your customer is already stressed, allow them to vent.

The Stress and Burnout Scenario

We have given you many *Super Service* tips on how to relieve stress and burnout—breathing, taking a break, or repeating affirmations. In this chapter, we are going beyond tips. Here, we are giving you keys to *prevent* stress and burnout from happening in the first place. First, let's take a close look at the cause of stress and burnout.

Let's say you are having a so-so day, not bad, not good. You get an irate customer; you handle it. Your boss is angry; you handle it. You get another angry customer; you handle it. A coworker wants help with a problem she should be able to solve by now; you handle it. You have lunch, the food is terrible, and everyone is talking about a TV show you didn't see. You feel isolated.

Back on the job, your boss is after you for something that was not your fault; you take it personally! Another customer calls with a complaint. You don't have the authority to solve it, so you pass it along to your manager who is annoyed at the disruption.

It's nearing the end of your day, and your boss asks you to stay and finish something up. Finally, you leave work. You feel miserable.

By the time you get home, you feel:

- *Either* lonely because no one is around,
  or confined because too many people are around.
- *Either* upset because there is no one to talk to,
  or frustrated because you have to listen to others' problems.
- *Either* depressed because you have nothing to do,
  or anxious because you have too much to do.

Whatever your scenario, you feel miserable. You wake up the next day, say an affirmation, and go to work. The same things happen—angry boss, irate customers, and inconsiderate coworkers.

This scenario continues until it becomes a chronic situation. You are drowning in an ongoing cycle of stress and burnout. You feel the only way out is to get another job.

You find a new job, but soon the same things start happening. You become so stressed and so burned out that you decide on a complete life change. You buy a plane ticket and fly away to a beautiful island and get a new job.

Life is great for the first few months. Then you notice a person who is angry, just like your old boss used to be! Your coworkers leave you out of conversations. Your customers complain for no reason. Stress and burnout are in your life whatever way you turn!

We have deliberately painted the worst-case scenario. All the same, maybe one or two things strike a chord with you and you do experience stress and burnout from time to time.

Let's get back to the high-wire performer and the forest. What do these two things have in common?

Answer: The stress and burnout had nothing to do with them. They just happened to be in the path. They felt at the mercy of the wire or the fire.

Do you see how that happens? The high-wire performer was just doing what high-wire people do. The forest was just being a forest. Then along came stress and burnout, and both were destroyed in the path.

Coping with Frustration

If you are really angry at someone, the only person that you can be sure is really suffering is you. It is like the breakup of a relationship. One partner usually feels the hurt more than the other. While the unhappy person is ranting and raving about his lost partner, the lost partner is happily taking care of herself. For most of us, voodoo dolls don't work, except on ourselves! When we feel anger and hatred, *we are the ones feeling it*. We are the ones being hurt. If this does not sound true, think about it for a moment. If there is conflict in your life, who is creating the conflict? Whether the conflict is between yourself and another person or within your department, if you are not creating it, you are probably feeding it! There is no one else.

The solution is to let go of our feelings and serve the customer. It doesn't mean that you must lose your own identity, or that you are "stuck" with someone else in your space. We have free choice to move where and when we will.

Control Your Environment

Let's go back to the work scenario. The angry boss, the irate customer, the inconsiderate coworkers, the inadequate home life—all of these things are outside your control.

Or are they? Our friend Mary works as an advertising copy writer. Mary is of short stature. At 41 inches (3 feet 5 inches), she is about the same height as a three-year-old child. Mary walks with the aid of crutches, drives a car, is always bright and cheerful, and has one of the most positive attitudes on the planet. Could she be stressed or burned out? Absolutely. It takes longer for her to walk to places. She depends on strangers to open and close doors, push elevator buttons, and on and on. Intrigued about her stress and burnout levels, we asked her if we could interview her for this chapter. She said yes!

Gees: "Do you ever feel stressed and burned out?"

Mary: "Oh, yes. It can be very stressful at times."

Gees: "But you always seem so happy; how do you avoid the stress and burnout?"

Mary: "I visualize the situation I'm going into. I foresee possible stressful situations and I address those fears beforehand. It's like heading them off at the pass."

Gees: "Can you give us an example?"

Mary: "If I'm meeting with a client, I think of ways to not make bad things happen. I call a cab way in advance so that I get there on time. I call to find out if the place is accessible or, if not, whether they can have someone assist me. I introduce myself over the phone and make friends with that person beforehand."

Gees: "Anything else?"

Mary: "I always give myself a reward when I've gone through it."

Gees: "How do your customers handle your being a little person?"

Mary: "I used to not tell them that I was 41 inches tall, but I found it shocked some customers. Others would say, 'I wish I had known: I would have done this or that for you.' For example, one customer now has a cushion in her car, so that I can sit higher up."

Gees: "So making the customer comfortable helps your stress level?"

Mary: "Oh, yes. I always do research ahead of time. I find the 'vibe' of the office. How are things run? What is their culture? Then I fit in with them."

Gees: "What happens when you meet a customer for the first time?"

Mary: "I had Montgomery Ward as a client and I was dealing with their fashion buyers in New York. Eventually I went there on a business trip and one of the men I had talked with every day on the phone invited me to a show and dinner. I asked all my friends, should I tell him about my stature or not? Some said yes, some said no. I ended up telling him and he was confused at first, and then said, fine, he was 6 feet 4 inches tall. We had a great time, he carried my purse."

▼

KEY POINT

Mary foresees stressful situations and takes care of them before they arise. Then she rewards herself for having done a good job.

You may think that your situation is not so simple, that you don't have time to plan and organize the way Mary does. Your customers come at you hard and fast. Sometimes you can't duck! You don't have time to visualize the situation. You can't head them off at the pass.

This is not true! If you have been in your job for a few days, you know what kind of customers you have. You know what kind of boss you have. You know what kind of coworkers you have. You *can* foresee situations. You *can* foresee stress. You *can* foresee burnout. You *can* plan how to handle them.

The problem is that most of us take everything so personally. We see ourselves as at the mercy of other people. The high-wire breaks and we fall. The fire blazes and we burn. If we remember that we do not have to walk the wire or stand in the path of a blazing fire, we can avoid the stress and burnout. Here are some tips.

Rules for Avoiding Stress and Burnout

Below are rules to help you avoid stress and burnout:

1. Identify the stressful situation.
2. Identify solutions.
3. Plan how to bring your solutions into effect.
4. Plan your reward.

CHECK-IN

Use one sentence to describe the most stressful situation in your job at this moment:

_____

_____

Write out two solutions that will help the situation:

1. _____

2. _____

Choose the most effective solution that will bring the strongest and most lasting results. Explain, in 10 words or less, how and when you plan on putting this into practice.

_____

_____

_____

_____

_____

Write down your reward. Choose something that you really enjoy, that doesn't cost a lot of money or take too much time.

_____

_____

_____

_____

A SUPER SERVICE PRAYER

May I walk with the desire to serve

May I open my heart to the needs of others

That my soul will leap in the joy of helping

That my circle of friends will grow with harmony

May I feel at one with the universe, one song for all

That my ego be fulfilled in the service of others

That my needs be filled by the joy of assisting

That my wants are turned into giving

And my desires turned into golden caring

May abundance of health, wealth, and happiness be mine

Coming from this desire to serve

This openness of heart

This joy of soul

Thank you, wondrous creator, for all my blessings

And may I learn to count them every day

And know that I am never alone.

Super Service—Final Words to End on . . .

You decide how you are going to live your life all the time. Every day you have choices on which way you want to go. You have the power to make or break organizations. You are the value-added. It is your attitude, the way you come to work every day, and the things you do that make the difference.

As soon as you become conscious, aware, and focused, wonderful things begin to happen. It's the strange thing of life; the buck actually does stop at you. We have this strange notion that senior people know more than we do, but they are also sitting in their offices wondering what to do. They need communication to go forward, so it is back to, what do you bring to the table? Are you walking the walk?

Is it better when it comes from management down? Yes, it is much better when it comes down. Most people need direction; they need to know where they are going. What are you contributing as an individual? What is your attitude when you walk to work every day? Are you contributing to the positive side or the negative side? What did you do to invest your time toward a good purpose? Decorate your office or cubicle with things to help you remember that you are a human being, that you are here to serve, and that you should be the best you can be.

We would like to leave you with a little reminder. When you deliver *Super Service*, the person feeling the best is you. So what is one thing, starting tomorrow morning, that you can do every day that will make a difference? Remember, one small step for you—one huge leap for *Super Service*.

Index

Acceptance, 15, 42, 44
Accountability, 18
Achievement, 117, 135
Action(s), 19, 36, 61, 73–74, 102, 114, 128, 138, 158
  achieving goals and, 117
  blame and bad, 123–124
  customers and, 46, 155
  daily, 47
  IKTA and, 116
  take, 115–128
  thoughts and, 73, 120–121
Adrenaline, 184
Advanced customer service skills, 139–199
  burnout and, avoiding, 183–199
  selling skills, 159–169
  stress and, avoiding, 183–199
  telephone skills, 171–181
  unhappy customers, handling, 141–158
Affirmations, 16–17, 43, 60, 119, 190–191
  positive, 119
  Super Service, 34, 44
  telephone skills, 178
Agreement, 94
  customer's proposal and, 99
  diversity and, 95–96
  reach, 91–102
Amiable customers, 145–146
Amway, 80–81
Analytical customers, 145–146
Anger, 16
  bodily effect of, 65–67
  customer, 143–145
  letting go of, 43
  preventing, 73
Apologizing, 150
Appreciation, 78, 130. *See also* Thankfulness

Assertiveness, 168
Attention, 69
Attitude, 43, 52, 57–60
  bad, 52–53
  changing, 20
  communication and, 55–56
  customers and, 71–72, 151
  personal life events and, 40
  positive, 51, 56, 57, 61
  right, 51–61
  service, 21, 54
  welcoming, 54–55
Awareness, 30, 109–110. *See also* Self-awareness
Awkwardness, handling problems and, 110

"Bad" events/situations, 40–41
Behavior, 20, 21, 122
Being your best, 42, 59
Blame, 123–124
Blue, releasing tension through color, 188
Body, 11, 66–67
Body language, 69–70
Boredom, 116
Brain, 2, 10–21
  animal, 11–13, 15, 18, 66
  human, 11, 13, 15, 18, 19
  immune system and, 67
  reptilian, 11
  reticular activating system in, 14
Breathing, 172–173, 185
Burnout, 192–193, 197
  avoiding, 183–199
  foreseeing, 195–196

Caring, 10
Cerebral cortex, 11, 13

Check-ins, 18, 35, 60, 89, 101, 114, 127, 137, 157, 169, 197
Choices, making different, 17–18
Collections, communication and, 143
Color therapy, 188, 189
Commitments, 39–40, 42, 80–81, 113
Communication, 39, 123, 125, 126, 135. *See also* Language
    attitude and, 55–56
    barriers, 156
    clear, 75–89
    collections and, 143
    customer, 28, 69, 112–113, 155–156
    customer service, 55–56
    KISS, 83–86
    listening and, 69
    mirroring and, 82–83
    positive, 118–119
    Super Service, 39, 75–89
    technical terms and, 84–85
    techniques, 69–70
    telephone skills and, 176, 177
    training, 143
    wording, 81, 86–87, 118–119
Competition, 97
Complaints, 25, 132, 154
Completing projects, 117–118
Computer use, telephone skills and, 180
Consequences, 94
Creativity, 99–100
Cross-selling, 160
CSR. *See* Customer service rep
Customer(s), 19, 26–27, 42–43, 57, 67, 68, 89, 111–113, 157
    actions, 46, 155
    angry, 143–145
    animal brain response to, 12
    attitude of, 71–72, 151
    choice of, 174
    communication with, 28, 69, 112–113, 155–156
    complaints, 25, 154
    connecting with heart and soul of, 9–36
    "deserving," 43–44
    difficult, 132
    educating, 107–109, 134
    expectations of, 110–111
    external, 35
    feelings and, 29, 31–32, 87–88
    great, 30, 33

    green, 150
    happy, 151
    helping, 92
    human brain response to, 13
    input of, 114
    interactions with, 29, 67–68
    internal, 19, 35
    irate, 156–158
    listening to, 10, 88, 150
    losing, 25–27
    "moments of truth," 27–28
    overpromising, 100
    personality types, 145–147
    profitability, 111
    red, 150
    relationship with, 19
    reports from, 145
    satisfaction, 97, 133, 144
    solutions and involving, 87, 91, 149, 153
    stress, 192
    treatment of, 96
    understanding, 67
    "undeserving," 43–44
    unhappy, handling, 141–158
    venting, 153–154, 192
    yellow, 150
Customer needs, 10, 38, 64, 67–68, 142, 160
    buying environment and, 65
    clarifying, 71
    honesty and, 73
    listening with open mind and, 68–70
    meeting, 71
    understanding, 63–74, 108
    upselling and, 64–65, 161
Customer service, 10, 20, 37–47, 54, 77–78, 106. *See also* Advanced customer service skills
    communication flow and, 55–56
    energy and, 106
    evaluating, 46
    follow-up, 125
    market differentiation and, 56–57
    personalizing, 112
    smiling and, 38, 54
Customer service rep (CSR), 163

Deep breathing, 185
Depression, 15
Desire to serve, 41, 43, 58–59
Desires, 71
Diversity, 95–96

Doing a good job, 5
Donations, 81
Driver customers, 145–146

Educating customers, 107–109, 134
Effect questions, 166
80/20 principle, 131–132
Emotion, 12, 18, 66–67. *See also* Feelings
Empathy, 153
Energy, 11–12, 23, 33, 104–107, 176
    customer service and, 106
    positive, 5, 33, 58, 61
    relationships and, 104
    selling skills and, 167–168
Environment, 19, 65, 194–196
Expectations, managing customer, 110–111
Explaining, 130
Expressive customers, 145, 147
Eye contact, 45, 54, 69

Favors, giving/getting, 79
Fear, 12
Feelings, 5, 16, 37–47
    customer, 29, 31–32, 87–88
Fight-or-flight, 12, 66, 109
Focus, 47, 69, 168
Focusing, 187
Follow-up, 125
Friendliness, 64
Front line, on, 134–137
Frustration, 194

Giving, 21–22
Goals, 80, 93, 108–109, 117
Good news/bad news approach, 87
Goodness, looking for, 117
Gratitude journal, 19

Habits, 110
Happiness, 57–58
Heart, connecting with, 9–36
Helpfulness, 42, 64, 77, 92, 134
Honesty, 73, 83–84

IKTA (I know that already) disease, 2, 10, 116–118
Immune system, 65–67
Improvement, areas for, 36
Information, giving, 83–87

Integrity, 113
"Internal dialogue," 56

Jargon, 84–86
Judgments, 44

Keep It Simple and Sincere (KISS), 75, 83–86

Labeling technique, 79–80
Language, 84, 147
Law of Attraction, 131
"Let go, let flow," 42
Limbic system, 11–13
Listening, 56, 70, 73, 76, 104, 130
    communication and, 69
    to customers, 10, 68–70, 88, 150
    negotiating and, 98
    open minded, 68–70
    telephone skills and, 173
Looking at the big picture, 92
Loosening tensed muscles, 185
Love, human brain and, 15

Manager, calling in, 88
Media, negative, 144
Meditation, relaxation and, 187
Mirroring, 82–83
Mistakes, 45, 73, 86
"Moments of truth," 27, 28
Mood, lifting, 59
Motivation, 80

Nail down questions, 166
Needs, 70–71
Negative comments, 144
Negative thoughts, 21–22, 40, 119–120
Negatives, 118–119
Negotiating, 98
Note taking, 173

Oak tree meditation, relaxation and, 187
Objectivity, 153
Off/on brand, 172
Open mind, 68–70, 92
OPEN technique, 165–166
Opening questions, 165
Opinions, 95–96
Outbound relationship building, experiment, 24–25

Outcomes, expected, 94
Ownership, taking, 47

Patience, 72
Persistence, 168
Personal life events, 39–41
Personality, 61
    customer, 145–147
Politeness, 64
Positive Mental Attitude, 57
Positive philosophy on life, 3
Positive thoughts, 21–22, 43
Positives, 118–119
Power, 95, 97
Praise, 117
Preparing for your day, 59
Probing questions, 165–166
Problem solving, 71–72, 89
Problems, handling, 109–110
Product or service profile, 85–86
Profanity, use of, 147
Profits, 97, 111
Progress reports, 123
Projects, finishing, 117–118
Promises, reaching agreement and, 100
Proposal, building on customer's, 99

Quality, 52
Questions, 165–166

Red Line, 181
Red, releasing tension through color, 189
Relationships, 19, 94, 104
Outbound relationship building, experiment, 24–25
Relaxation, 184–186
    exercises, 186–191
Releasing tension through color blue, 188
Releasing tension through color red, 189
Reservations, motivation for people to keep, 80
Respect, customer, 10
Responsibility, 18, 45–46, 72, 86, 114, 134, 147
Reticular activating system, 14
Right thought, 120–121

Satisfaction
    building on, 129–138
    customer, 97, 133, 144
Saying yes, 76–77

Self-awareness, 111
Self-confidence, 191
Self-esteem, 191
Selling, 164, 167–168
Selling skills, 159–169
    energy, 167–168
    OPEN technique, 165
    questions, 165–166
    upselling, 160–164
Service, 4, 39–40, 52, 164. *See also* Advanced
        customer service skills; Customer service;
        Desire to serve; *Super Service*
    attitude and, 21, 54
    definition of, 20
    profile, 85–86
    selling and, 164
Service providers, 2–3, 66
Six sales situations for solutions, 164
Smiling, 19, 21, 59, 83
    customer service and, 38, 54
Solutions, 89
    customer involvement in, 87, 91, 149, 153
    possible, 95
    six sales situations for, 164
    win-win, 96–99
SOP. *See* Standard Operating Procedure
Standard Operating Procedure (SOP), 109–110
State of mind
    being in charge of, 17
    choosing, 57–58
    maintaining positive, 57–59
Step outside yourself, 43–44
Stone, W. Clement, 57
Stress, 197
    avoiding, 183–199
    controlling environment and, 194–196
    customer, 192
    foreseeing, 195–196
    frustration and, 194
    relaxation and, 184–186
    relieving, 190–191
    scenario, 192–193
String incentives, 78–79
Success, 137, 138
Super Service, 5
    action, taking and, 115–128
    affirmations, 34, 44
    attitude, 51–61

Super Service (Cont'd.)
    bottom line of, 24–25
    check understanding and, 103–114
    communication and, 39, 75–89
    customer needs and, 63–74
    delivering, 43, 49–138
    example of, 3–4
    giving, 65–66
    how am I doing, 36
    lives enriched by, 2–3
    as positive philosophy on life, 3
    practicing delivery of, 5
    reach agreement and, 91–102
    satisfaction and, 129–138
    self-assessment tool/results, 29
    service providers and, 2–3, 66
    value of, 24–25
    workouts, 34–36
Survival, 66

Taking, 21–22
Taking breaks, 22–23
Taking things personally, 59, 70, 88
Technical terms, 84–85
Telephone skills, 171–181
    affirmations, 178
    communication and, 176, 177
    computer use and, 180
    effectiveness, 177
    listening and, 173
    messages, 175–176, 180
    Red Line for internal use and, 181

    transferring a call and, 179
    voice and, 176–177
Thankfulness, 47, 123, 132
Thinking/thoughts, 16, 21–22, 60. *See also* Negative
    thoughts; Positive thoughts
action and, 73, 120–121
Three brains, 2, 10–21
Tipping, 78
Trade, 93
Trust, 82
Truth, 73, 150

Understanding, 67
    check, 103–114
Updates, 123
Upselling, 2, 160–164
    cross-selling *v.*, 160
    customer's needs and, 64–65, 161
    do's/don'ts, 162
Urgency, 153

Value(s)
    added, 131–132, 136
    processed, 133
    Super Service, 24–25
Venting, customer, 153–154, 192
Visualization techniques, 17, 69, 174

"What-goes-around-comes-around," 33
Win-win solutions, 96–99
Wording, 81, 86–87, 118–119
Writing things down, 80–81, 93